# Cultural

Theory and History
Series Editor: Donald M. MacRaild

**Published**

# Cultural History

Anna Green

First published 2008 by
PALGRAVE MACMILLAN
Houndmills, Basingstoke, Hampshire RG21 6XS and
175 Fifth Avenue, New York, NY 10010
Companies and representatives throughout the world

PALGRAVE MACMILLAN is the global academic imprint of the Palgrave Macmillan division of St. Martin's Press, LLC and of Palgrave Macmillan Ltd. Macmillan® is a registered trademark in the United States, United Kingdom and other countries. Palgrave is a registered trademark in the European Union and other countries.

ISBN-13: 978–0–333–98674–5     hardback
ISBN-10: 0–333–98674–1          hardback
ISBN-13: 978–0–333–98675–2     paperback
ISBN-10: 0–333–98675–X          paperback

This book is printed on paper suitable for recycling and made from fully managed and sustained forest sources. Logging, pulping and manufacturing processes are expected to conform to the environmental regulations of the country of origin.

A catalogue record for this book is available from the British Library.

A catalog record for this book is available from the Library of Congress.

10  9  8  7  6  5  4  3  2  1
17  16  15  14  13  12  11  10  09  08

Transferred to Digital Printing in 2010.

# Contents

# Preface

Cultural history is a very broad and eclectic field, in terms both of subject matter and of theoretical perspectives. It covers a great variety of topics, it does not revolve around one particular theory, and different national and cultural contexts have generated diverse historiographies. This poses a major dilemma for the author attempting to construct a coherent introduction to the field. Rather than take the reader on a 'Cook's Tour' of cultural history as a whole, this book unpacks a complex body of work to reveal the major theoretical strands. It provides an entry into those theories and concepts widely deployed within cultural history, draws some connections between them, and identifies the major questions that have preoccupied cultural historians from the nineteenth century to the present.

At different times, friends and colleagues at the University of Waikato drew relevant or interesting texts to my attention, or discussed difficult conceptual issues with me, and I would like to thank Peter Gibbons, Cathy Coleborne, Liz McKinley, Alexandra Barratt, and Rowland Weston. The external readers also provided helpful comments. I would like to acknowledge a research grant for this project from the Faculty of Arts and Social Sciences at the University of Waikato. Finally, may I thank Merryn Williams for permission to use an extended quotation from the work of Raymond Williams.

The lengthy gestation of this book would have tried the patience of a saint, and I am most grateful to the editors at Palgrave Macmillan and the series editor for their unflagging support. The same must be said for Jack Vowles, whose encouragement, and interest in the theoretical debates, contributed to the pleasure of writing this book.

A.G.

# Introduction

The idea of culture sits at the heart of cultural history. Despite its widespread use in everyday communication, and perhaps because of its centrality to a range of academic disciplines such as anthropology, sociology, literary criticism, cultural history and cultural studies, the concept of culture remains complex and contested. If it is impossible to define culture, can we establish any parameters around the field of cultural history? Peter Burke outlines the problem and proposes one way out of the dilemma:

> Over forty years ago, two American scholars set out to chart the variations in the use of the term in English, and collected more than two hundred rival definitions. . . . In the search for our subject it may therefore be appropriate to adapt the existentialists' definition of man and to say that cultural history has no essence. It can only be defined in terms of its own history.
>
> How can anyone write a history of something which lacks a fixed identity? It is rather like trying to catch a cloud in a butterfly net.[1]

Because culture has so many definitions and meanings Burke infers that it is impossible to reach a definitive or overarching interpretation. Therefore, he argues, if it is impossible to establish a common definition of culture, it is equally impossible to define cultural history. Burke concludes that the only way to define cultural history is by its own history.[2] But he then appears to say that this *too* is impossible, utilizing a wonderfully evocative metaphor, which appears to catch the insubstantial and fleeting nature of cultural history – one minute you seem to see a clear shape, in the next it has dissolved or re-formed. Is cultural history as difficult to define as Burke's metaphor suggests, and why have historians been unable to reach any sort of agreement?

## ► Defining 'culture'

E. P. Thompson was quite right to point out that culture is a 'clumpish term', one which gathers up 'many activities and attributes into one common bundle'.[3] This may not matter when culture is being used in a broadly descriptive sense, but the bundle needs to be unpacked if we are to establish any theoretical focus in the field of cultural history. Let us begin, drawing upon the influential cultural theorist Raymond Williams, by reviewing the etymology of the word 'culture' in the English language.[4]

The word originally described the act of cultivation in husbandry – the tending of crops or animals. From the sixteenth century onwards, the word was applied not only to husbandry but also to the 'process of human development', gradually expanding to describe the intellectual, spiritual and aesthetic dimensions of human society and history. Then, in the late eighteenth and early nineteenth centuries, culture acquired an additional or alternative meaning to that of civilization and progress. Partly in resistance to the changes being wrought by industrialization, Romantic writers focused upon national and folk cultures – the social, lived practices among different groups of people. This shift in focus had a particular outcome: culture became pluralized into cultures, which varied over time and place, and among social groups, and this fatally undermined the previous conception of a singular, unilinear process of human development (in which European civilization was perceived to represent the apex of achievement). By the late twentieth century, culture came to have three principal meanings: 'a general process of intellectual, spiritual and aesthetic development; a particular way of life, whether of a people, a period, a group, or humanity in general [and] . . . the works and practices of intellectual and especially artistic activity.'[5]

The origins and meanings of culture include both 'symbolic' and 'material' production. This dualism reflects two long-standing philosophical positions within western thought: the first, known as the 'idealist', focuses upon the world of the human mind, with an 'emphasis on the *informing spirit* of a whole way of life . . . most evident in specifically cultural activities – a language, styles of art, kinds of intellectual work'. In contrast, a 'materialist' position argues that cultural activities arise within a social context including, for example, social relationships and economic production, and that these fundamentally shape cultural expression.[6] This philosophical dualism between the mental world of ideas and symbolic expression, on one hand, and that of the social and material context on the other is reflected in the debates within cultural history.

Cultural historians studying the expression of human beliefs, emotions and values have moved between these two positions at different points in time. Most historians have turned, at least in part, to the social or economic context to explain the origins of specific cultural beliefs and practices.[7] Cultural Marxists, for example, continued to emphasize the importance of exploitative economic relationships and the processes of production in working-class cultural history. In the 1980s, however, the influence of poststructuralism turned this relationship on its head. Poststructuralist historians replaced economic or social determination with that of language: semiotics and discourse. Social and cultural historians began to focus on the ways in which ideas of 'class' were expressed, rather than the social and material contexts of production in which class relationships were embedded. These positions, Marxist and poststructuralist, reflect the two poles of the debate within cultural history over the respective significance of the material and the symbolic in human culture.

Many historians and cultural theorists, however, prefer a more interactive model of human consciousness. In 1988 the French cultural historian Roger Chartier suggested that the human mind and the world of social and economic structures existed in a mutually constitutive relationship.[8] More recently the literary theorist Terry Eagleton made a similar argument, reminding us that the origins of the concept of culture lie in the practice of human husbandry, entailing both 'regulation and spontaneous growth'. These dual dimensions, he suggests, indicate a rejection of extreme positions: 'Human beings are not mere products of their environs, but neither are those environs sheer clay for their arbitrary self-fashioning. If culture transfigures nature, it is a project to which nature sets rigorous limits.'[9]

The ideal/material, or mind/matter, dichotomy is, however, only one of a number of dualisms that permeate human thought. These dichotomies are based upon difference or oppositional characteristics, and there are three that have generated recurrent debates among cultural historians. In addition to the mind/matter dichotomy above, the conscious/unconscious dimensions of human subjectivity, and elite/popular cultural expression, constantly surface within all fields of cultural history. More specific binary oppositions within language (enshrining essential characteristics) have also generated rich historiographies. The distinction between male and female, for example, is central to psychoanalytic, gender and poststructuralist historiography; and the occidental/oriental, to postcolonial cultural histories. Dualisms and binary oppositions such as these are diffused throughout human thought and linguistic structures, and it is difficult for cultural historians to escape the practices of comparison and dichotomization.[10] One such attempt to overcome this dimension of language, through the deconstruction of binary oppositions, will be found in the chapter on poststructuralism and discourse.

Does the sheer breadth of human activity encompassed within the diverse elements of culture, mental and material, elite and popular, preclude a coherent focus for the field of cultural history? Many areas of cultural activity are now specialized subjects, such as the history of art, ideas, or law. Is cultural history simply the sum of a wide number of sub-fields? Is it possible to distinguish cultural history from social history, or are cultural historians in general interested in the material or social context, and in various forms of social analysis, just as social historians are aware of the influence of ideas? If we look at the history of cultural history it could be argued that there are three unifying strands that, at a broad level, characterize the field. The first is a focus upon human subjectivity, and the creative dimensions of the human mind; the second, a holistic approach to culture that seeks to identify the unifying structures, patterns or systems that connect the whole; and thirdly, an interpretive, hermeneutic, method of analysis. In these ways cultural history is much more than the sum of its parts, and at various junctures, departs from social history. Let us look at these three aspects of cultural history in turn.

## ► Human subjectivity

The first defining feature of cultural history is its focus upon human subjectivity and the creative dimensions of the human mind. Human beings make sense of their world in a myriad of ways. Through the evidence of symbolic systems, material culture and social practice, cultural historians over the past century and a half have sought to reveal the underlying, conscious or unconscious, human mind and its conceptual frameworks, beliefs and myths. From the nineteenth-century concept of *zeitgeist* to the twentieth-century notion of discourse, cultural histories concentrate upon the world created by the human mind. Cultural history, therefore, can be defined as an approach to the past that focuses upon the ways in which human beings made sense of their worlds, and this places human subjectivity and consciousness at the centre of cultural enquiry.[11] This broad definition permits us to gather within its compass the many activities and attributes generally ascribed to culture, while retaining the essential focus upon the creative dimensions of the human mind. Many approaches within cultural history look for the unconscious, underlying and unifying basis of cultural expression, and the principal intellectual metaphor of social and cultural theory over the nineteenth and twentieth centuries has been that of structures.

As with culture and cultural history, definitions of structuralism are difficult, since it is 'a loose, amorphous, many-faceted phenomenon with no clear lines of demarcation'.[12] In the following discussion a distinction will be made between structuralist perspectives, and structural_ism_ as a movement. Early theorists of structure, using the term in the first, broader sense, would include Karl Marx and Sigmund Freud, as well as the linguist Ferdinand de Saussure. What these theorists held in common was:

> a conviction that surface events and phenomena are to be explained by structures, data, and phenomena below the surface. The explicit and obvious is to be explained by and is determined – in some sense of the term – by what is implicit

and not obvious. The attempt to uncover deep structures, unconscious motivations, and underlying causes which account for human actions at a more basic and profound level than do individual conscious decisions, and which shape, influence, and structure those decisions, is an enterprise which unites Marx, Freud, Saussure, and modern structuralists.[13]

Structural theorists in this broad sense have had a widespread impact – both direct and indirect – upon cultural history. A brief survey of the last fifty or so years demonstrates their influence: the continuing presence of psychoanalytic approaches to history from about 1960 onwards; the body of Marxist cultural history in the 1950s and 1960s, followed by the anthropological and literary influence of the 1980s; and finally the poststructuralist 'linguistic turn' from the 1990s onwards. Each of these phases drew upon the explication of a psychological, social, symbolic or linguistic structure or system shaping and constraining (or even determining) the expression of human consciousness.

Structuralism as a movement is usually confined to linguistic structuralism, particularly influential among some French anthropologists and literary theorists from the 1960s onwards.[14] The influence of this approach upon cultural history is explored further in Chapter 4, but it is useful to note here two distinctive features of structuralism. First of all, understanding is based upon the form, not upon the content. The consequence of this approach is to displace meaning onto the structure; a narrative, for example, is explained by the structure of the story rather than the content or meaning. Secondly, the discrete elements of a narrative or image can only be understood in relation to each other. The analysis rests upon the 'structure of relations between the units'.[15] However, not all theories that employ the metaphor of structure necessarily share these specific characteristics. The common ground among structuralist perspectives may be found in the assumption that deep social, psychological, symbolic or linguistic structures fundamentally shape, or in some cases determine, human subjectivity.

But there is no consensus among historians regarding the specific nature or structure of human consciousness that governs the ways in which human beings have made sense of their worlds. In terms of theorization, cultural history could be best described as a search for grand theory, sometimes realized (psychoanalysis, Marxism, semiotics) but more often limited to particular concepts. The broad field of cultural history is distinguished from its smaller sub-specialities by its search for theoretical frameworks and analytic concepts – the building blocks of theory – that combine diverse expressions of human consciousness at a given time into patterns or networks of meaning. This leads us to the second strand that characterizes the field of cultural history: the emphasis upon collective frameworks of thought.

## ▶ Holistic approach

A holistic approach to culture, with an emphasis upon collective modes of thought, is evident from at least the mid-nineteenth century. The origins of cultural history may be traced back through eighteenth-century philosophy and histories of literature, language and painting, which developed along different lines, including separate terminologies, in first the German, and later the French, national contexts. By the mid-nineteenth century, *Kulturgeschichte* was well established in Germany as both a popular genre and a scholarly discipline.[16] Out of this fertile intellectual context emerged the Swiss-born cultural historian Jacob Burckhardt, whose writings on cultural history and cultural analysis raised many of the fundamental conceptual and epistemological issues that both unite the field of cultural history, and pose its most consistent problems.

Burckhardt published his widely acknowledged masterpiece *The Civilization of the Renaissance in Italy* in 1860. He defined the task of the cultural historian as revealing the mind or spirit, the characteristic 'habits of thought and mental attitudes', of a society or civilization, a focus that has strong undertones of the Hegelian concept of *Zeitgeist*, or the unifying spirit of an age. Burckhardt argued that imagination, aspirations and assumptions are at least as important, if not more so, than actions or events for the cultural historian. Since these aspects of the past, he continued, are conveyed unintentionally and unconsciously through historical sources, the work of the cultural historian was therefore far superior to histories based upon the potentially deceptive evidence and ephemeral world of purposeful human action. Burckhardt's approach to cultural history explored the multifaceted nature of human consciousness through a search for unifying, deeper patterns of thought revealed unintentionally in the historical evidence. This is a strong common denominator in the work of cultural historians over the past century and a half.

The search for underlying collective modes of thought, so apparent in the work of Burckhardt, is also evident in the French school of history known as the *Annales*, established in the 1920s by Lucien Febvre and Marc Bloch. Drawing upon the work of the French philosopher Lucien Lévy-Bruhl, they brought the concept of *mentalité* into wider circulation. Until recently the terms *mentalités collectives, civilisation*, or *imaginaire social*, rather than 'culture', have dominated French cultural history.[17] While there is considerable confusion over the meaning of the term, Febvre defined *mentalité* in terms of the mental tools or equipment available to individuals at any given time, and through which they made sense of the world. These tools could be linguistic, conceptual, or affective, but the precise configuration at a specific point in time gave shape to that era's *mentalité*.[18]

The centripetal tendencies of *zeitgeist* and *mentalités* were reinforced by theories and approaches from sociology and anthropology that were also widely influential among cultural historians. The theorist Émile Durkheim (1858–1917), the founder of the discipline of sociology, devoted his life to establishing a science of society. Durkheim gave the study of the social group or community precedence over that of the individual, believing that human behaviour is fundamentally shaped by the moral, religious and social precepts of the society in which the individual lives. Furthermore, he argued that rituals and ceremonies within societies performed the vital function of creating social cohesion and stability. With its emphasis upon the functional aspects of social behaviour, this organic metaphor of society also implied that all aspects of society were interrelated and that society should be studied as a whole. The influence of Durkheim will be found in many of the concepts and theories within cultural history, from *mentalités* to collective memory.

Earlier, in 1871, Edward Burnett Tylor, a key figure in the foundation of anthropology as an academic discipline, defined culture as 'that complex whole which includes knowledge, belief, art, morals, law, custom and any other capabilities and habits acquired by man as a member of society'.[19] The key words in Tylor's definition are 'that complex whole': in his definition only biology was excluded from a comprehensive list of disparate elements. A century later, in 1961, the virtues of a holistic approach to the study of the past were emphasized by one of the first British historians to borrow from anthropology, Keith Thomas.[20] By this stage, many American anthropologists, in particular, had jettisoned the institutional and organizational aspects of Tylor's definition and approached culture as the symbolic expression of a system of ideas.[21] Cultural historians in the 1980s, for example, were greatly influenced by the work of the anthropologist Clifford Geertz, who expanded upon the symbolic dimensions of culture in his 1973 study *The Interpretation of Cultures*. This emphasis upon the shared, symbolic aspect of human culture preceded the development of the 'linguistic turn' within the humanities, with its emphasis upon the role of language in mediating human expression. By the end of the twentieth century, the focus upon unconscious, collective and symbolic forms of cultural expression became the dominant approach among cultural historians.

There are a number of potential pitfalls in the holism of *Zeitgeist, mentalité,* and symbolic systems. These approaches characterize culture as a 'bounded, coherent collectivity', as the anthropologist James Clifford pointed out in a seminal book, at the expense of dissent and conflict:

> The inclusive twentieth-century culture category . . . this culture with a small c orders phenomena in ways that privilege the coherent, balanced, and 'authentic' aspects of shared life. Since the mid-nineteenth century, ideas of culture have gathered up those elements that seem to give continuity and depth to collective existence, seeing it whole rather than disputed, torn, intertextual, or syncretic.[22]

An exclusive focus upon cultural cohesion makes it difficult to account for cultural change, and this has been one of the major charges against cultural history. The predominantly synchronic focus of cultural histories, the elaboration of cultural structures or beliefs at a particular moment in time, also contributes to this problem. Those schools of cultural history that retain a stronger materialist and diachronic orientation, as we shall see, have been more successful at explaining cultural change. For example, Marxism is based upon the dialectic of economic and social conflict. While the Marxist historian E. P. Thompson rejected economic reductionism, the physical experience of exploitative economic relationships played a central role in his account of the development of working-class consciousness. In Thompson's work, cultural change was the product of both the material transformation in human productive relationships, and individual and collective intellectual and moral *agency*. But cultural theories that posit the autonomy of symbolic systems and discourse have greater difficulty explaining the change from one pattern or system of thought to another.[23]

Finally, the last question arising out of a holistic approach to culture concerns the status of the individual, and the concept of the 'self'. The search for the shared, cohesive aspects of culture results in an inescapable tension within cultural history. First of all the sources utilized by cultural historians are nearly always generated by the individual hand or voice, and the relationship between individual subjectivity and collective beliefs and behaviour remains central to cultural analysis and interpretation. Over the past century and a half, cultural historians have moved from a position exalting the individual elite voice, to one that largely submerges the individual within shared linguistic, social and cultural structures. In 1977, Raymond Williams rejected both extremes, opposing any approach that exclusively elevated the individual author, or that denied any possibility of 'individual initiative, of a creative or self-generating kind'.[24] He argued that the relationship between social language or signs and individual 'inner' consciousness needed 'further radical exploration', but with only a few exceptions cultural historians have not followed this direction. Nonetheless, the value of the individual voice lies in its ability to illuminate the range of 'expressive possibilities' within a culture.[25] This is evident, for example, in Carlo Ginzburg's *The Cheese and the Worms*, which explored the ways in which the sixteenth-century miller Mennochio thought about the society and the wider world within which he lived. Mennochio's ironic commentary, emotions and imagination, carefully situated within the wider cultural and social context, are at the centre of Ginzburg's narrative and greatly expand our understanding of the 'expressive possibilities' of the time.[26]

In contrast, poststructuralists perceive the individual as a discursive construction, and reject the making of human consciousness as a creative, active, and reflexive process. Some have gone further, and argue that the mistaken construction of the self as a coherent and independent subject in modern Western thought should be the central question for cultural history.[27] Definitions of selfhood are complex, but intellectual historians usually circle around three dimensions: 'the material or bodily, the relational or social, and the reflexive or self-positing'.[28] It is on the last of these dimensions, the capacity of individuals to recognize and critically reflect upon their own consciousness, that active human agency ultimately depends. This is an essential component of Marxist (or post-Marxist) conceptualization of human agency, for example, from Antonio Gramsci to Pierre Bourdieu. Traditionally historians of 'elite' cultural history, such as intellectual history or the history of art, have acknowledged the ability of individuals to engage critically and creatively with inherited perspectives; those writing about popular culture – with the exception of cultural materialists – have been much less sure.[29]

## ▶ Interpretive methodology

This brings us to the third dimension of cultural history, the interpretive approach and its corollary, a relativist approach to historical truth. In contrast to many of his disciplinary contemporaries, Burckhardt drew attention to the mediating role played by the historian's own subjectivity in shaping accounts of the past. Placing a great deal of emphasis upon scholarly intuition, Burkhardt suggested that the Renaissance might well present a very different picture to another historian. Wilhelm Dilthey, an important nineteenth-century theorist of intellectual and cultural history, shared the same relativist position, although not the emphasis upon intuition. The historian's subjectivity, Dilthey argued, was a positive resource for historical methodology, although he spent his life trying to find a way to put the interpretive practice of cultural history on a defensible epistemological foundation. For both these nineteenth-century historians cultural history was a matter of **representation**. Historical evidence, as well as the historian's own account of the past, should be understood as representations, rather than reconstructions, of reality.

Central to all forms of cultural history, therefore, is the process of symbolic mediation through which human beings make sense of their world. 'Representation' is one way to describe how this is done, and may be broadly defined as 'the construction of meaning through signs and concepts'.[30] But how does the cultural historian understand and interpret the figurative language and symbolic representations of very different cultures and societies in the past? In the last fifty years, two broad research paradigms have shaped the social sciences: the first modelled upon the natural sciences, and the second derived from an interpretive hermeneutic tradition.[31] It is the latter that has dominated the thinking of cultural historians. Dilthey characterized the hermeneutic approach as the search for understanding or meaning, in contrast to the search for origins, causes, or explanation that dominated nineteenth-century empiricist historiography. The twentieth-century philosopher Paul Ricoeur (1913–2005) took this a step further, defining the hermeneutic interpretive approach as the process of 'deciphering the hidden meaning in the apparent meaning, in unfolding the levels of meaning implied in the literal meaning.'[32] At the core of the hermeneutical approach, therefore, is the belief that it is possible for the historian to understand those who lived in the past in ways that they themselves could not have expressed or understood.[33]

## ▶ Conclusion

These, then, are the three intertwined strands of cultural history: the focus upon human subjectivity; a holistic approach to culture that seeks to identify the unifying structures, patterns, or systems that connect the whole; and an interpretive, hermeneutic approach. In the search to understand human subjectivity, cultural historians have been eclectic, drawing in particular from literary theory, psychology, anthropology and linguistics. In the next six chapters we will explore the fully fledged theories of psychoanalysis, Marxism and linguistic structuralism/post-structuralism, as well as the major concepts, *Zeitgeist,* hermeneutics, *mentalités,* the unconscious, agency, symbolism, gender, narrative, discourse, remembering, and collective memory, that have shaped the writing of cultural history over the past century and a half.

# 1 *Zeitgeist* and Hermeneutics

During the nineteenth century the writing of history became a professional academic discipline. And, almost from the beginning, a divergence in theory and method created two parallel strands of historical research: political history, and cultural history. In the turbulent context of European nationalism in the nineteenth century, and the rise of nation-states, most historians focused upon political history and the history of events. The theories and methods that emerged from this school of historians were to define the discipline until the latter half of the twentieth century. It is useful to begin this chapter with the major principles of this dominant school of historical enquiry because these provided a set of codified practices against which other late nineteenth-century, and twentieth-century, historians defined their own approach to the study of the past. Without awareness of this wider intellectual context, it is difficult to understand the meditations of cultural historians on the nature of historical research.

Leopold von Ranke, at the University of Berlin, was the leading figure in this field, and between 1824 and 1871 he developed professional standards for historical training. The core principles of Ranke's scientific, empirical history rested upon two key assertions. First of all, it was possible for historians to put aside their *a priori* beliefs, and engage in impartial research. Consistent with this position Ranke also rejected any role for theory, arguing instead for an inductive method of reasoning, from the particular to the general. However, a specific theory of knowledge, or **epistemology**, is reflected in these principles. First, the past exists independently of the individual's mind, and is both observable and verifiable. Secondly – through rigorous examination of the evidence – it is possible for the historian to reconstruct the past objectively and accurately. A generation of historians were trained at Berlin, and empirical research methods became the bedrock of the historical profession. They underpin the search for objective truth, 'the noble dream' of the historical profession.[1]

The empirical methods institutionalized by Ranke reinforced a broader underlying principle emphasized by the influential Romantic scholar Johan Gottfried Herder (1744–1803): that all societies and cultures, every historical period, should be understood on its own terms, not through the moral lens of the historian. This approach became known as 'historicism', and represented a definitive break with previous traditions of historical understanding. Until the early nineteenth century, historians approached their study of the past on the assumption that human nature was constant, and that the past could reveal exemplars for human behaviour in the present. Historicism decisively broke with this unified perspective, proposing in its place a history of diverse human societies and cultures, each with its own set of social structures and cultural beliefs.[2] This perspective was widely shared among historians in the later nineteenth century, and indeed it is argued that 'most educated people in the West have been in some sense historicists, for they believe that their lives, both individual and collective, take shape in time, now conceived as a universal, secular continuum'.[3]

Cultural historians shared the belief in the diversity of cultures and societies, but in other respects diverged quite fundamentally from the scientific, empiricist political historians. In the nineteenth century, cultural histories were polarized around the two extremes of a cultural history spectrum. At one end were descriptive accounts of daily life and folklore; at the other, the history of human civilization and progress reflected through the writings and aesthetic production (paintings, music, architecture) of great thinkers and artists. It was from the latter group of cultural historians that the first challenge to aspects of Ranke's scientific history emerged. In this chapter we will look at three of the most significant figures in nineteenth- and early twentieth-century cultural history: Jacob Burckhardt, Wilhelm Dilthey and Johan Huizinga. All three were imbued with the 'philosophic tradition of German historicism with its emphasis upon human consciousness'.[4] The questions they raised about the nature and methods of cultural history resonate among historians still.

## ▶ Jacob Burckhardt (1818–97)

The son of a clergyman in Basel, Switzerland, Jacob Burckhardt originally intended to follow his father's footsteps and become a Protestant minister. However, while studying theology in Basel he came to the conclusion that Christianity was a **myth**.[5] Turning instead to the study of history and art history, he spent four years studying with Leopold Ranke in Berlin. Burckhardt's relationship with Ranke is the subject of contrary points of view among historians. Some argue that Burckhardt retained a high regard for Ranke throughout his life, despite their differences, which were fundamental. While Ranke saw the 'power of the state as guardian of order and stability, Burckhardt regarded power as tied to evil. Ranke, the Protestant scholar, confidently sought the hand of a benevolent God in the events of the past; but Burckhardt, skeptical and withdrawn, saw in history an unending struggle between antagonistic forces.'[6] These differences led other historians to argue that we should not be misled by Burckhardt's references to Ranke as 'my great master'. Rather, Burckhardt came to reject both Ranke's personal ambition and his intellectual approach.[7]

By 1842 Burckhardt had decided that he would devote his life to cultural history (*Kulturgeschichte*).[8] He returned to Switzerland, initially combining journalism with lecturing at the University of Basel. After some publication successes, he was awarded the chair of history at Zurich Polytechnic, where he taught for three years before returning to the University of Basel.[9] Despite offers from Munich, Göttingen, Tübingen and Berlin (to succeed Ranke), Burckhardt elected to remain at Basel. The decision to remain at a provincial university, it has been argued, reflected Burckhardt's distaste for contemporary politics. He was conservative by tempera-ment and conviction, and witnessing the revolutionary years of 1846–52 had left him with the desire to withdraw from contemporary society and politics.[10]

During his life, Burckhardt wrote three great works of cultural history: *The Age of Constantine the Great* (1852); *The Civilization of the Renaissance in Italy* (1860); and *Greek Cultural History* (published posthumously in 1898). Of these, *The Civilization of the Renaissance in Italy* is considered to be his masterpiece, and according to contemporary historians continues to 'stimulate much of the most creative schol-arship in late medieval and early modern European history . . . it has become a classic, compelling each new generation of readers to come to terms with its argu-ments'.[11] Written in 1860, it was first translated into English in 1878. The six parts of the book focus upon the following themes: 'The State as a Work of Art'; 'The Development of the Individual'; 'The Revival of Antiquity'; 'The Discovery of the World and of Man'; 'Society and Festivals'; and 'Morality and Religion'. It did not, as might have been expected, include art or architecture, for Burckhardt intended to write a separate volume on these, a goal subsequently only partially fulfilled.[12] Through the six themes outlined above, Burckhardt described a society in which a new awareness of the individual was taking root: this, he suggested, represented the unifying spirit of the Renaissance.

Burckhardt's metaphorical description of the Renaissance as the discovery of the human individual became 'one of the most powerful metaphors that have ever been proposed in all of the history of historical writing'.[13] This **metaphor** is encap-sulated in the following passage from *The Civilization of the Renaissance in Italy*:

> In the Middle Ages both sides of human consciousness – that which was turned within as that which was turned without – lay dreaming or half awake beneath a common veil. The veil was woven of faith, illusion and childish prepossession, through which the world and history were seen clad in strange hues. Man was conscious of himself only as a member of a race, people, party, family or corpora-tion – only through some general category. In Italy this veil first melted into air.[14]

In this visually arresting passage, Burckhardt demonstrates the importance he placed upon human consciousness and its capacity for change, leading in this case to the emergence of individuality, a sense of self.

The task for the cultural historian, Burckhardt explained, in the introduction to *The Greeks and Greek Civilization,* is to understand 'the history of Greek habits of thought and mental attitudes, and to seek to establish the vital forces, both constructive and destructive, that were active in Greek life', in particular looking for their 'essential peculiarities'. The goal of his study is 'the history of the Greek mind or spirit'.[15] In an important passage, emphasizing the contrast with event-based political narrative history, Burckhardt defined the strengths of cultural history:

> Cultural history by contrast possesses a primary degree of certainty, as it consists for the most part of material conveyed in an unintentional, disinterested or even involuntary way by sources and monuments; they betray their secrets unconsciously. . . . This kind of history aims at the inner core of bygone humanity, and at describing what manner of people these were, what they wished for, thought, perceived and were capable of. In the process it arrives at what is constant, and finally this constant comes to seem greater and more important than the ephemeral, and qualities greater and more instructive than actions. . . . Desires and assumptions are, then, as important as events, the attitude as important as anything done.

Burckhardt makes it clear that the goal of the cultural historian is to seek what is 'constant and characteristic' in the beliefs and values of a particular society. How could these be identified? He advised his students that only 'long and varied reading can give assurance.'[16]

Burckhardt challenged more than the focus of historical enquiry, however. In contrast to the empiricists' belief in impartial, objective historical writing, he suggested that historians brought their own perceptions to the process of research. He accepted that other scholars might well see the Renaissance differently, and describes his book as 'an essay in the strictest sense of the word'. E. H. Gombrich reminds us that 'essay' means literally an attempt, an experiment, a try-out'.[17] This is Burckhardt's intention: to emphasize that his work is a tentative and subjective representation of the past. Indeed, he comments that, 'outlines of a cultural period and its mentality may present a different picture to every beholder, and the same studies which resulted in this book might easily have led others to essentially different conclusions'.[18] Burckhardt was fully aware that individual perception, or human subjectivity, played a significant mediating role in the historian's representation of the past.

'I lay no claim to be "scientific" and have no method, at least none shared with other scholars', Burckhardt told his students.[19] Much earlier, when still a student himself, he wrote to a friend:

> you will have to concede to me the following – a person such as myself who is quite unsuited to speculative theorizing and who never, even for a minute in a whole year, feels disposed towards abstract thought, such a person will do best if he attempts to approach the higher questions of life and of research in his own way and tries to clarify these issues as best he can.[20]

Despite his rejection of 'speculative theorizing', Burckhardt was nonetheless influenced by the ideas circulating among nineteenth-century scholars and thinkers. Let us examine some of the ways in which Burckhardt drew upon the ideas of contemporary philosophers.

## ▶ *Zeitgeist*

The first issue concerns Burckhardt's desire to reveal the 'spirit of a culture'. Intrinsic to this goal is a holistic assumption that all aspects of social and cultural activity and expression are linked through underlying patterns of thought or belief, a position that owes a great deal to the philosopher George Hegel (1770–1831). Central to Hegel's historicism was a belief in the homogeneity of a particular culture: 'that each society is a unique whole, all of whose parts are inseparable from one another. The art, religion, constitution, traditions, manners, and language of a people form a systematic unity.'[21] Collectively these constitute the *Geist*, or spirit, of the society.[22] Burckhardt's approach clearly reflects a belief in *Zeitgeist*, the spirit of an age, and this shaped his analysis of diverse cultural sources. In taking disparate aspects of Renaissance culture and social activities, and finding in each the same expressions of the spirit of individualism, Burckhardt adopted 'the Hegelian construct of cultural history with its corollary, the "exegetic method"'. This is an interpretive approach based upon the assumption of 'essential structural similarity' in all the various dimensions of social and cultural life in a particular society.[23]

On the other hand, unlike many German historians, Burckhardt's analysis of the past rested upon a framework of political and cultural conflict. In a series of lectures, published after his death as *Reflections on History*, Burckhardt spelt out his conceptual approach. He identified three eternally contending fundamental forces of history: state, religion and culture. The state, he argued, desired power most of all: 'the idea is to make the general will of the nation felt abroad, in defiance of other nations'. Power, Burckhardt stated without qualification 'is of its nature evil, whoever wields it'.[24] In this he was entirely opposed to Ranke, who perceived the rise of the nation-state as the working out of God's will for mankind. Nor was Burckhardt any more inclined to see the second force, that of religion, in a more positive light. The major world religions, he argued, entertained similar ambitions to dominate the world and the individual.[25] Only culture, 'in perpetual flux', could be free from the restrictions of state and religion. Culture, he suggested, is:

> the sum of all that has *spontaneously* arisen for the advancement of material life and as an expression of spiritual and moral life – all social intercourse, technologies, arts, literatures and sciences. It is the realm of the variable, free, not necessarily universal, of all that cannot lay claim to compulsive authority.[26]

Burckhardt's identification of three antagonistic forces driving history diverged from the perspective of many of his peers, including Hegel and Ranke, who saw them as complementary and interdependent. Culture, according to Burckhardt, could only thrive when the coercive powers of state and religion were diminished and could no longer inhibit the culture's 'innermost impulses'. The Renaissance was one such moment.[27]

Let us look at an example of Burckhardt's exegetic method, and the ways in which he draws out the connections between cultural beliefs and activities. In the chapter on 'Morality' in *The Civilization of the Renaissance in Italy,* he examines in turn sentiments of honour, the exercise of imagination, the practice of *vendetta,* and attitudes towards adultery or crimes such as murder. Burckhardt discovers in each of these evidence of the 'excessive individualism', the unifying *Zeitgeist,* of the Italian character during the Renaissance. The chapter concludes:

> The individual first inwardly casts off the authority of a state which, as a fact, is in most cases tyrannical and illegitimate, and what he thinks and does is, rightly or wrongly, now called treason. The sight of victorious egoism in others drives him to defend his own right by his own arm. And while thinking to restore his inward equilibrium he falls, through the vengeance which he executes, into the hands of the Powers of Darkness. His love, too, turns mostly for satisfaction to another individuality equally developed – namely, to his neighbour's wife. In face of all objective facts, of laws and restraints of whatever kind, he retains the feeling of his own sovereignty, and in each single instance forms his decision independently, according as honour or interest, passion or calculation, revenge or renunciation, gain the upper hand in his own mind.[28]

This passage supports the contention that Burckhardt was 'deeply ambivalent' about the development of individualism.[29] While culture represented the least coercive realm of human interaction, his pessimistic temperament permitted few illusions concerning the trajectory of history.[30]

## ▶ Representation, pessimism and the 'ironic vision'

This brings us to a second influence upon Burckhardt, this time one he acknowledged, that of the philosopher Arthur Schopenhauer (1788–1860).[31] Born in Danzig, a generation earlier than Burckhardt, Schopenhauer exercised a considerable influence over conservative intellectuals in the mid-nineteenth century.[32] His ideas appealed to those without sympathy towards the goals and activities of contemporary radical movements and who, as a consequence, predicted disastrous outcomes from the destruction of the old political order. This reflected Burckhardt's position: 'I know too much about history to expect anything from the despotism of the masses but a future tyranny, which will mean the end of history,' he wrote to a contemporary.[33] Schopenhauer's philosophy provided the intellectual justification for Burckhardt's withdrawal from active political and public life.

Schopenhauer's ideas influenced Burckhardt at two related levels: **epistemology**, and mode of historical writing. To take epistemology first, Schopenhauer, following the philosopher Immanuel Kant, was a **transcendental idealist**. The material world, for Schopenhauer, is not an illusion, nor simply a matter of mental construction. But he draws a distinction between material reality and its appearance to humankind; in other words, 'the world of our representations is the only world we know – and the only world we can ever know.'[34] The key concept is that of *Vorstellung*, most frequently translated as 'representation'.[35] This distinction between 'representations' and 'reality' is the key to Schopenhauer's philosophy.[36] The origins of Burckhardt's emphasis upon the place of subjective perception, including intuition, imagination and empathy in shaping historical representation, and his insistence upon the provisional and personal nature of his study of the Renaissance, may be found in Schopenhauer's emphasis upon the concept of 'representation'.

A second powerful inheritance from Schopenhauer was a pessimistic view of human society and history. Schopenhauer's whole system of thought 'was a sustained attempt to show why social concerns and historical interests are unnecessary'. Life was 'terrible, senseless . . . all apparent communities are delusions; all pretense of love is a fraud; all apparent progress in the creation of manifestly more human understanding is sheer myth'.[37] This view of the world is reflected in Burckhardt's historical writing where 'virtue was usually betrayed, talent perverted, and power turned to service of the baser cause'. Haydn White suggests that this represents an ironic vision of human history:

> The linguistic mode of the ironic consciousness reflects a doubt in the capacity of language itself to render adequately what perception gives and thought constructs about the nature of reality. It develops in the context of an awareness of a fatal asymmetry between the processes of reality and *any* characterization of those processes. . . . In the end, it conceives the world as trapped within a prison made of language, the world as a 'forest of symbols'. It sees no way out of this forest, and so it contents itself with the explosion of all formulas, all myths, in the interest of pure 'contemplation' and resignation to the world of 'things as they are'.[38]

White argues that Burckhardt liberated the nineteenth century from the dominant myths of history popular in his own age, those of Romance, Comedy and Tragedy. In their place he elevated the myth of Satire, 'in which historical knowledge is definitively separated from any relevance to the social and cultural problems of its own time and place'.[39]

However, Burckhardt did seek enduring insights into the human condition from his studies in literature and art. In this he was, once again, influenced by Schopenhauer, who argued that the object of philosophy lay in the 'unchangeable and in what lasts, and not in the things which are now like this, and now again like that'.[40] Burckhardt believed 'that it is in the sphere of culture that human contemplation can perceive that spiritual *continuum* which . . . gives meaning to all history'.[41] The richest sources for evidence of this spiritual continuum were the myths and images, poetry and philosophy passed down over time. In the introduction to *The Greeks and Greek Civilization*, Burckhardt reminded us that we still 'see with the eyes of the Greeks and use their phrases when we speak'.[42] Understanding this enduring 'life of the mind' is why, for Burckhardt, cultural history would always be more important than the transient events of human political history. 'Artists, poets and philosophers have a dual function,' he wrote, 'to give ideal form to the inner content of time and the world and to transmit it to posterity as an imperishable heritage.'[43]

## ▶ Wilhelm Dilthey (1833–1911)

In a review of *The Civilization of the Renaissance in Italy*, the young Wilhelm Dilthey took issue with aspects of Burckhardt's approach. While acknowledging particular strengths in Burckhardt's characterization of the period, Dilthey criticized the opacity of the conceptual framework and the reduction of diverse phenomena to a 'not fully plausible universal image':

> But the comprehensive concepts he uses to try to express its meaning are so general in themselves, and also so little explained by him, that they serve more to etherealize the phenomenon than to define it in a clear intuition.[44]

Finding a way to clarify the interpretive practice of cultural history, and place it on a sound epistemological footing, was the task Dilthey set himself. Although more sympathetic than Burckhardt to the goals of the scientific empirical method, Dilthey also challenged aspects of Ranke's empirical and historicist approach. He argued that the practice of writing history, drawing as it does upon diverse forms of human expression and communication, was not amenable to the same explanatory methods employed in the natural sciences. New methods needed to be found so that historical analysis could achieve a similar degree of reliability to that accorded the natural sciences.

Dilthey studied theology at the University of Heidelberg, and philosophy and history at the University of Berlin. During his lifetime he published intellectual history and biography, as well as *Introduction to the Human Sciences* (1883), and *Hermeneutics and the Study of History* (1910), although most of his writings were published after his death.[45] The gradual emergence of Dilthey's voluminous body of work was accompanied, for English scholars, by an even slower process of translation into English; for example, by 1961 still only a fraction of Dilthey's work was available.[46] In contrast, comprehensive Spanish translations were published in the mid-1940s.[47] This may explain the relative neglect in the English-speaking world of this important theorist of cultural and intellectual history.

Dilthey spent much of his lifetime trying to resolve intractable questions relating to historical epistemology. In the following discussion of the theoretical and methodological problems that so preoccupied him it is worth bearing in mind that Dilthey's writings have been characterized as a maze, without clear structure or process of development.[48] Let us begin the difficult task of creating a coherent account of Dilthey's contribution to cultural history by contextualizing his work within the nineteenth-century German scholarly environment that stimulated his intellectual quest. Once again, a significant early influence was Leopold von Ranke. Like Burckhardt, Dilthey had also attended Ranke's lectures at the University of Berlin, and while he agreed with many of the aims and methods of historicism, Dilthey thought the methodology as a whole lacked a sound philosophical basis.[49] Nineteenth-century historicists sought to reveal the ways in which people thought in the past, their beliefs, feelings, and imaginings, in order to understand their intentions and actions. The epistemological questions and problems associated with this approach were clearly articulated by Dilthey. The first was this: if the historian's goal is to reconstruct the past on its own terms, how were historians to understand the lives and thought of people so very different from themselves? 'How', Dilthey asked, 'can one quite individually structured consciousness bring an alien individuality of a completely different type to objective knowledge through such re-creation?'[50]

## ▶ Understanding (*Verstehen*)

The concept of understanding, or *Verstehen*, became central to Dilthey's work. However, there is substantial disagreement among scholars over Dilthey's use of the terms 'understanding' and 'interpretation', for at times he appears to use them interchangeably. It has been argued that the problem lies in the complicated course of Dilthey's thinking over his lifetime, and that after 1882 he 'revised his conception of knowledge of the human world . . . to know the human world is not an act of *Verstehen* of man's experiences, but an act of *interpretation* – a "*hermeneutic*" act . . . '.[51] However, in the following passage, taken from 'The Rise of Hermeneutics' written in 1900, Dilthey appears to suggest that a process of 'understanding' precedes the development of interpretive systems:

> All interpretation of written works is merely the rule-guided working out of the process of understanding that pervades our whole life and pertains to every kind of speech and writing. The analysis of understanding is therefore the groundwork for the codification of interpretation.[52]

Dilthey's concept of understanding has been defined as the 'disclosing the "inner core" of human action . . . [and] "the nature of its agency"'.[53] Understanding human actions in the past could not be achieved with the scientific methodologies of his time, Dilthey argued, because the natural world is very different from the world of human thought and behaviour. 'We explain nature', he wrote, 'but we understand mental life.' Human beings communicate: therefore the historian's understanding (*Verstehen*) is 'the process of grasping what is conveyed to us by words, gestures, and the like'.[54] More than one hundred years later, similar distinctions between theories applicable to the human and natural worlds are still being made.[55]

Dilthey distinguished between three levels of historical understanding. First, there is the 'chronicler, who has an "epic interest" in the narrative configuration of events'. Secondly, there is the 'pragmatic historian, who has an interest in the political motivations behind the affairs of state'. And finally, the third level is that of 'the universal historian, who "has the task of reconstructing the whole of inner life"'. Dilthey belonged to the last category of historian, writing individual intellectual biographical studies of Schleiermacher, Leibniz, Frederick the Great, and Hegel. Dilthey's search for understanding, therefore, was very different from Hegel's concept of the *Geist,* or spirit of an age. *Verstehen* did not consist of intuitively identifying an essence of a culture; rather, understanding drew upon knowledge of the reciprocal patterns of relations between the individual and the social, economic or cultural context. Dilthey suggested, as an example, that Bismarck should be understood by studying the diverse 'coherences' of his life, such as 'family, state, religion, legal system, class, generation, and culture, which define his role as historical agent'.[56] The individual represented the intersection of multiple cultural and material influences.

However, like Burckhardt, Dilthey argued that historical understanding was inevitably reflected through the perspective of the interpreter. In the *Introduction to the Human Sciences* (1883) Dilthey criticized Ranke for his wish 'to efface himself in order to see things as they were'.[57] According to Dilthey, the historian drew upon both imagination and reflective judgement: 'the first condition for the possibility of a *Geschichtswissenschaft* (history as a discipline) lies in the consciousness that I am myself a historical creature, that the one who examines history also makes history.'[58] This is what makes Dilthey seem so contemporary: the emphasis he placed upon the historian's relationship with the past through re-creation and identification. He was the first to recognize the value of sympathy (*Mitfühlens*) and empathy (*Einfühlung*) as cognitive tools in historical research, and the way he conceptualized a historian's subjectivity was, R. G. Collingwood declared in 1956, 'a great advance on anything achieved by any of [his] German contemporaries'.[59]

Dilthey therefore considered that the historian's understanding would always be relative and never fully definitive, one reason why he has long been regarded as the 'archrelativist' by critics.[60] The problem of subjectivity and perspective preoccupied most nineteenth- and twentieth-century thinkers. Dilthey responded to these questions by adopting and developing the concept of *Weltanschauung*, or world-views. A *Weltanschauung* encompasses the 'overall perspective on life . . . the way a person perceives the world, evaluates and responds to it'. Each of us, according to Dilthey, needs to make sense of our life in the form of an 'over-arching orientation or interpretation . . . which in turns conditions our further conduct of life.'[61] Dilthey developed a typology of three kinds of *Weltanschauungen*: naturalism, subjective idealism, and objective idealism, 'reflecting the dominance of either the feeling, the willing, or the intellectual aspects of consciousness'.[62] While *Weltanschauungen* were historically produced, influenced by time and place, they also derived from the 'deepest attitudes of personality', and in particular the inclination towards optimism or pessimism.[63] By combining the theory of *Weltanschauungen* with a formal method of textual analysis, Dilthey sought to achieve a 'unified approach to understanding the meaning of historical life'.[64] His goal remained consistent: to establish 'the system of presuppositions which justifies the judgement of historians . . . and provides criteria for establishing that they are true'.[65] However, the epistemological problems of understanding human expression and communication in a method comparable to 'universally valid science' were immense.

## ▶ Hermeneutics

Dilthey turned to the analytical methodology of hermeneutics, first used by the Ancient Greeks to interpret poetry. Hermeneutics concerns the principles of textual interpretation that are applied to establish the meaning, or understanding, of texts.[66] Expropriated by theology for the interpretation of religious manuscripts in later centuries, hermeneutics had expanded to the study of a much wider range of written texts and forms of expression by the nineteenth century.[67] Dilthey's hermeneutic approach to the study of the past analysed both events and society through the beliefs and intentions of those present and active at the time.

Central to Dilthey's interpretive approach is the concept of the 'hermeneutic circle', a term he took from the philosopher and theologian Friedrich Schleiermacher (1768–1834).[68] In the hermeneutic circle there are many layers of interpretation, each of which is circular in nature. Dilthey suggested that the hermeneutic circle consisted of 'three relationships of mutual dependency: between single words and the totality of the work, between the work itself and the mentality of its author, and between the work and the literary **genre** to which it belongs'.[69] First of all, textual clarification depends upon the reader moving back and forth between parts of the text and the whole. However, the circular movement also expands beyond the text itself. The historian must also consider the broader context within which it was constructed – for example, comparison with other contemporaneous texts. This juxtaposition of texts, sometimes involving the comparison of very different genres, is a feature of contemporary intellectual history. Secondly, the interpreter also exists within an enclosed circular relationship with the text. Interpretation is always, Dilthey wrote, reflective "to a certain degree" of the experience of the interpreter. That is, there is a 'mutual dependency between the historian's life-experience and his interpretation of the past'.[70] Within the circle, however, there is no absolute starting point, or point of certainty upon which to construct an interpretation. All our understandings have to be regarded as provisional and capable of revision.

The central problem associated with the notion of the hermeneutic circle is that it assumes a certain coherence and unity within the text. The focus upon the author's intentions, central to Dilthey's approach, implies that the work should be regarded as an 'integrated whole'. There is, of course, no reason why this should be the case. Texts from the past may be 'diffuse, incomplete and internally contradictory', and authors may have had multiple, or contradictory, intentions.[71] Dilthey chose to focus upon intellectual biography but, as we saw earlier, he was well aware of the physical and collective dimensions of human life. He accepted that other methods were required to investigate historical factors external to the human mind, and understood that hermeneutics worked in cooperation with empirical research.[72] But his search for understanding, rather than explanation, meant that his biographies focused much more upon the cumulative development of ideas, and in particular the perspective individuals attached to their own lives:

> As meaning is rooted in the interpretations and plans that an individual superimposes on his own doings and the things that happen to him, an outside interpretation of his life must start from and take account of the meaning he has given to his own life. . . .[73]

Although Dilthey's writings were only translated slowly into English, through the German sociologist Max Weber and the British philosopher and historian R. G. Collingwood he exercised an indirect influence upon intellectual historians writing in English in the latter half of the twentieth century. Aspects of Dilthey's approach, for example, resonate in a seminal article published by the intellectual historian Quentin Skinner in 1969.[74] In the article Skinner described the two conventional approaches adopted by historians of ideas: the first interpreted the text within the wider social, economic or political context, while the second focused exclusively upon the text itself. Skinner argued, in contrast, that the intentions of the author were the key to understanding textual meaning. Texts, he suggested, should be understood as acts of rhetorical communication and therefore historical interpretation was primarily a linguistic exercise. Skinner's approach reflected Dilthey's insight that a text could only be understood in light of the author's intentions. The question of intentional meaning is also integral to Paul Ricoeur's reflections upon hermeneutics. However, Ricoeur expands the scope of intentional meaning beyond that of the individual author into the wider culture. Exploring the meaning of texts that were not composed by a single author, such as the Bible or **myths**, Ricoeur was interested in the '*mode of intentionality* that accompanies the text, be it belief, repentence, remorse . . . '.[75]

But what about factors of which historical actors are unaware? One such factor, raised by the philospher and political scientist Jürgen Habermas (1929–   ), is that of unconscious motivation.[76] Habermas argues that hermeneutics could be given the rigorous basis Dilthey sought through an interpretive alliance with the principles of psychoanalysis. Sigmund Freud developed psychoanalytic theory in the early part of the twentieth century, and argued that adult human behaviour derived primarily from childhood sexual development and subsequent psychic conflict and repression within the unconscious mind. Habermas thought that the combination of scientific psychoanalytic principles with the hermeneutic approach could provide a fruitful analytic approach to the study of mankind. In modified and varied forms, later in the twentieth century, other cultural historians have taken this route, and their work is discussed more fully in a later chapter.

The influence of the historicist, hermeneutic interpretive approach is also evident in contemporary literary studies. The New Historicists rejected analyses that focused upon literary form alone and sought to bring an awareness of historical specificity to the process of understanding literary texts. Such an understanding, they argued, could not depend upon abstract principles or theoretical models, but relied upon 'an encounter with the singular, the specific, and the individual'.[77] This attraction to the single voice or event in the past is exemplified, for example, in the attention the group has paid to the anecdote.[78] Hermeneutical analysis was also taken in new directions, such as a less celebratory approach to canonical literary texts. Traditional **'close readings'**, it has been argued, were often conducted in a spirit of admiration and celebration of genius. This has been replaced by a more critical interpretive approach bearing, one practitioner acknowledged, an 'inescapable tinge of aggression, however much it is qualified by admiration and empathy'.[79] The work of the New Historicists has been criticized for failing to acknowledge broader historical patterns, and for collapsing historical knowledge into the perspective of the contemporary observer.[80]

On the occasion of his seventieth birthday in 1903, Dilthey acknowledged that he had not achieved his aim of solving the epistemological problems entailed in hermeneutic analysis:

> I undertook to examine the nature and condition of historical consciousness – a critique of historical reason. . . . An apparently irreconcilable antithesis arises when historical consciousness is followed to its last consequences. The finitude of every historical phenomenon – be it religion or an ideal or a philosophical system – accordingly, the relativity of every kind of human apprehension of the totality of things is the last word of the historical *Weltanschauung* (world-view). Everything passes away in the process; nothing remains. And over against this both the demand of thought and the striving of philosophy for universally valid knowledge assert themselves. The historical *Weltanschauung* liberates the human spirit from the last chains that natural science and philosophy have not yet broken. But where are the means to overcome the anarchy of opinions that then threatens to befall us? To the solution of the long series of problems that are connected with this, I have devoted my whole life. I see the goal. If I fall short along the way, then I hope my young travelling companions, my students, will follow it to the end.[81]

## ▶ Conclusion

Dilthey never really reconciled his sympathy for historicism with his desire to establish an irrefutable epistemological basis for human knowledge. Historicists argued that each period in history needed to be understood on its own terms. But both Burckhardt and Dilthey rejected Ranke's belief that historians could set aside their own perspectives, and simply write what actually happened, *'wie es eigentlich gewesen'*.[82] Burckhardt drew attention to the role played by the historian's intuition and imagination in historical representation, while Dilthey emphasized the circular relationship of text and interpreter, each enclosed within a particular *Weltanschauung* or consciousness. Both focused upon the political, cultural or intellectual elite. And each demonstrated, in different ways, the interrelationship between beliefs and values, and the material, social or political structures of society. In other respects the two historians differed. Whereas Burckhardt sought the collective spirit of the age, Dilthey rejected any totalizing system of thought and focused upon the individual as the nexus of cultural and social relationships. While Burckhardt explicitly chose to avoid confronting theoretical problems, Dilthey spent his life seeking to reconcile the subjectivity of the sources and the historian with the goal of objective historical knowledge. Subsequent generations of cultural historians were to wrestle with the questions and problems identified by Burckhardt and Dilthey in the nineteenth century.

Both Burckhardt and Dilthey primarily studied elite society and culture, and it was their most immediate successor, the Dutch historian Johan Huizinga (1872–1945), who argued that cultural history should be expanded to include the ordinary and the popular. Huizinga occupied professorial chairs at Groningen in 1905 and then at the University of Leiden; interned during the Second World War, he died shortly before its end in 1945. Huizinga argued that cultural historians should include the lives and perceptions of ordinary people. The objects of cultural history, he argued, 'are the manifold forms and functions of civilization as they can be detected from the history of peoples and of social groups, and as they consolidate into cultural figures, motifs, themes, symbols, concepts, ideals, styles and sentiments'. He suggested that historians should investigate cultural functions such as honour, obedience or resistance, as well as cultural sites such as the garden, the road, the market, or the inn. The role of cultural history was to demonstrate 'their constantly varying shapes and effects in different ages and different lands'.[83]

The extent to which Huizinga's historical writing reflected the lives of ordinary people was, however, limited. In his major work, *The Waning of the Middle Ages,* Huizinga sought to understand the spirit of the age, as Burckhardt had done, through the study of social activities and forms of visual and literary representation.[84] In this sense he continued to rely upon elite literary, religious and artistic sources to capture the 'medieval mind' of the fifteenth century. Chapters on chivalry, heroism, love, religious sensibility, and death, and on the power of linguistic and visual symbolic representation, include vivid evocations of the sounds, sights, sensations and cruel contrasts and insecurity of the medieval town. The power of Huizinga's representation of the Middle Ages lies, as it did with

Burckhardt, in his capacity to combine disparate and complex elements of medieval life into a unifying metaphorical image.[85]

Huizinga and Burckhardt share a number of common characteristics in their approach to the study of the past. Both rejected the scientific positivism of Ranke in favour of the historian's historical imagination and intuition. It is important to note the qualification that Huizinga 'did not mean that history is *only* imaginative, but only that imagination is indispensable in interpreting the past'. It was indispensable because aesthetic intuition 'paves the way for rational explanation'.[86] Secondly, Huizinga also relied upon the cultural activities and representations of the elite for his generalizations about medieval man, but he lacked the means to establish the relationship or correspondence between elite and popular culture, an enduring problem within cultural history.[87] In the next chapter we will consider the extent to which Huizinga's near contemporaries, the French historians of the *Annales* movement, were able to overcome this shortcoming in their studies of *mentalités*. How did they address the theoretical and methodological problems of understanding collective modes of thought in the past?

# 2 *Mentalités* and the Unconscious

One of the central tensions within cultural history concerns the conscious and unconscious dimensions of human thought and behaviour. Traditional intellectual history, or the history of ideas, investigates and contextualizes the conscious expression of ideas. Other forms of cultural history, however, have focused upon the underlying, unconscious, and collectively shared, aspects of human expression. This chapter will focus on the latter, looking at two quite distinct approaches to the study of the unconscious imperatives that shape human subjectivity, and drive human behaviour. The first, based on the concept of *mentalités*, originated with Marc Bloch and Lucien Febvre at the University of Strasbourg in the 1920s. The second approach is based upon psychoanalytic theory, and draws upon the work of Sigmund Freud and his successors.

Bloch and Febvre founded the *Annales,* named after the journal they established in 1929. Scornful of the emphasis upon narrative diplomatic and political history evident within orthodox French historiography, Bloch and Febvre preferred to 'deal with the problems posed by the reality of the past rather the problems posed by the documents'.[1] The new problem-oriented history of Bloch and Febvre required different questions, new kinds of sources, and the search for more adequate conceptualization. First of all, Bloch and Febvre rejected their contemporaries' focus upon the ideas of the elite and individual intellectuals, turning instead to the collective history of the whole of society. 'Not the man, never the man, human societies, organized groups', wrote Febvre in 1922.[2] In order to understand collective human behaviour and beliefs in the past, the *Annales* historians – again unlike their more orthodox contemporaries – actively drew upon the approaches of cognate disciplines, including anthropology, sociology, psychology, geography and linguistics, among others. 'Historians, be geographers. Be jurists too, and sociologists, and psychologists,' Febvre commanded in 1953.[3] The faculty structure at Strasbourg, unusually for the time, facilitated collaborative teaching and research, and Bloch and Febvre participated in interdisciplinary seminars at which scholars from a diverse range of fields presented their own research, or debated the literature, theories and methods current in their field.[4] Throughout their lives both men emphasized the productive engagement that historians could have with the social sciences.

## ▶ Definitions of *Mentalité*

The term *mentalité* came into wider circulation following the publication by the philosopher Lucien Lévy-Bruhl of *La mentalité primitive* in 1922.[5] Lévy-Bruhl argued that primitive peoples thought in a 'pre-logical' or 'mystical' way, and Febvre and Bloch 'developed the notion that beyond individual thinkers and their particular expressions of value and belief lay patterned systems of thought – "mentalities" – which differed radically from age to age.'[6] There have been a number of criticisms of the idea of mentalities. Many historians have found the concept of *mentalité* imprecise or ambiguous.[7] Others have queried the extent to which the concept of *mentalité* represents a change of direction, or advance, on the concept of *Zeitgeist*.[8] In contrast to *Zeitgeist*, however, the historian of *mentalités* shifts our attention to the mental structures through which human perceptions are conveyed. These structures include all the ways in which mental activity is shaped and expressed, through imagery, linguistic patterns, rituals or customs.[9]

Febvre defined *mentalité* as the *'outillage mental'*, the mental tools or equipment used by people in the past to make sense of their world:

> Every civilization has its own mental tools. Even more, every era of the same civilization, every advance in technology of science that gives it its character, has a revised set of tools, a little more refined for certain purposes, a little less so for others. A civilization or an era has no assurance that it will be able to transmit these mental tools in their entirety to succeeding civilizations and eras. The tools may undergo significant deterioration, regression, and distortion; or, on the contrary, more improvement, enrichment, and complexity. They are valuable for the civilization that succeeds in forging them, and they are valuable for the era that uses them; they are not valuable for all eternity, or for all humanity, nor even for the whole narrow course of development within one civilization.[10]

What did Febvre mean by mental tools? Roger Chartier suggests that 'in any given epoch, the criss-crossing of these various lines of support (linguistic, conceptual, affective) determines certain "modes of thought" that shape specific intellectual configurations (for example, the limits between the possible and the impossible or the boundaries between the natural and the supernatural)'. This definition of *mentalité* draws more upon psychological than intellectual categories. Chartier also identifies two important implications of Febvre's definition: first, that categories of thought are not universal (and certainly not reducible to contemporary ways of thinking); and secondly, that there is no continual or necessary progress in the succession of *outillage mental*.[11]

The history of mentalities, therefore, has three specific, and distinctive, features. First of all, as discussed earlier, historians of mentalities emphasize collective attitudes rather than those of individuals, and the thought of ordinary people, not simply the educated elites. Following from that, the focus is upon 'unspoken or unconscious assumptions, on perception, on the workings of "everyday thought" or "practical reason"', rather than conscious thought or clearly articulated theories. Finally, consistent with Febvre's concept of mental tools, historians of mentalities seek to understand the underlying structures of belief, 'the categories . . . metaphors and symbols, with how people think as well as what they think'. Consequently, it is argued that 'to assert the existence of a difference in mentalities between two groups is to make a much stronger statement than merely asserting a difference in attitudes'.[12]

## ▶ Collective consciousness

Let us turn to two foundational studies in the history of *mentalités*, beginning with Bloch's first major book, *Les Rois thaumaturges: étude sur le caractère surnaturel attribué à la puissance royale, particulièrement en France et en Angleterre,* published in 1924. It was not until 1973 that it was translated and published in English as *The Royal Touch: Sacred Monarchy and Scrofula in England and France.* Nominated as 'one of the great historical works of our century', it investigates the cultural phenomenon of the king's healing touch in both France and England.[13] The first chapter opens in 1340, with the English ambassador of Edward III seeking the support of the Venetians against the King of France, Philip of Valois. In his speech, the ambassador is reported to have proposed that the contest between the two kings be settled in the form of three trials. The first was personal combat, a duel between the two, or a small group of their loyal supporters. Secondly, 'if Philip of Valois is – as he affirms – the true king of France, let him prove the fact by exposing himself to hungry lions; for lions never attack a true king; or let him perform the miraculous healing of the sick, as all other true kings are wont to do' – meaning, no doubt, the 'other true kings of France'. Bloch reminds the reader that despite the fact this challenge was largely a diplomatic formality, the gulf between the ambassador's words and those of a contemporary diplomat should give us pause for thought.[14]

Bloch suggests that the ambassador's challenge reflects the 'collective consciousness' regarding royal sacred and miraculous powers, particularly those of healing people suffering from scrofula (tuberculosis). The term 'collective consciousness' is taken from the French sociologist and philosopher Émile Durkheim, who argued that 'the fundamental categories of human reason are collective representations'.[15] Scrofula was an endemic and disfiguring disease that left 'countless sufferers longing for healing, and ready to have recourse to any remedies they might hear of through common report.'[16] Bloch sought to understand the longevity and vitality of beliefs in the supernatural powers of the king to cure scrofula with the touch of his hand. Consistent with the *Annales'* focus upon the collective and social, rather than the individual and elite, one of Bloch's central questions concerns the acceptance by the general population of the royal claim to miraculous powers. In so doing, Bloch addresses the issue of correspondence between the culture of the elite and that of the common people. To what extent does Bloch successfully demonstrate this correspondence?

Bloch argues that 'men's minds were prepared to conceive or to admit' the practice of the royal healing power because the Christian world of religious miracles existed in a continuum with the earthly world in which they lived. 'Sacred actions, objects or individuals were thus thought of not only as reservoirs of powers available beyond this present life, but also as sources of energy capable of exerting an immediate influence on this earth too.'[17] Demonstrating a capacity for such beliefs among the wider population does not, however, explain why the rite took hold at a specific time and place. To answer this, Bloch turned towards more conventional political explanations. Bloch rejects the idea that the development of similar healing rites by the English kings a century or so later is mere coincidence. The healing rite, he suggests, originated in France in about 1000, and was 'plagiarized' with 'ulterior political motive' by English kings approximately a century later.[18] Bloch concludes by putting forward two hypotheses regarding the royal touch that link the exercise of political power with deeper collective beliefs:

> If an institution marked out for particular ends chosen by an individual will is to take hold upon an entire nation, it must be borne along by the deeper currents of the collective consciousness. The reverse is perhaps also true: for a rather vague belief to become crystallized in a regular rite, it is of some importance that clearly expressed personal wills should help it to take shape.[19]

In these ways, Bloch demonstrates interaction between broader cultural beliefs in religious supernatural powers, and the agency of kings anxious to strengthen the foundations of their political power.

Why did belief in the royal touch continue over eight centuries? Did not the failures undermine faith in the sovereign's miraculous powers? As Bloch commented, 'scrofula is not a disease that is easily cured: it often recurs over a long period, sometimes almost indefinitely; but it is pre-eminently a disease that easily gives the illusion of being cured; for its symptoms – tumours, fistulas, suppurations and the like – fairly often disappear of themselves, only to come back again later on at the same spot or elsewhere'. Many sufferers sought repeated laying-on of hands, and in England a superstition took hold that 'the royal touch was only really effective if repeated', and Bloch makes the point that 'this could only have come about through the first touch being often ineffective'. Complaints could be turned aside in a number of ways: the patient's lack of faith; an erroneous diagnosis; or the slow nature of the cure.[20] Furthermore, reflecting Febvre's *outillage mental*, Bloch argues that contemporaries simply lacked the 'critical powers' to mount a challenge. Their 'psychology of the miraculous' was, he concludes, a 'collective error', or 'collective illusion'.[21] This is the source of a criticism that is often directed against Marc Bloch and other cultural historians: that of making judgements about mentalities, of seeing some beliefs as more rational or modern than others.[22] Bloch's argument reflects the contrast between logical and prelogical thought originally proposed by Lucien Lévy-Bruhl, from which the idea of mentalities arose.

## ▶ The constraints of *outillage mental*

Let us turn to the second example from the history of *mentalités*, written during Lucien Febvre's exile in the countryside during the Second World War, and published in 1942. *Le Problème de l'incroyance au XVIᵉ siècle: la religion de Rabelais*, was translated and published in English forty years later as *The Problem of Unbelief in the Sixteenth Century: The Religion of Rabelais*. The title sums up Febvre's intentions: the principal purpose of the book is to explore the case against the novelist and philosopher Rabelais, accused of atheism and anti-Christian thought following the appearance of *Pantagruel* in 1532. However, this study, Febvre insists, is not a monograph on Rabelais, but an 'essay on the meaning and spirit of the sixteenth century'. A central theme running throughout *The Problem of Unbelief* concerns historical anachronism, the tendency of later writers to assume a retrospective continuity and comparability in ideas concerning 'unbelief', and to find the origins of 'free thought' in the sixteenth century.

> The problem is in knowing how men in 1532 heard *Pantagruel* and *Cymbalum mundi*, how they were capable of hearing and comprehending them. Let us turn the sentence around. It is, even more, in knowing how those men were absolutely incapable of hearing or comprehending them. We instinctively bring to bear on these texts our ideas, our feelings, the fruit of our scientific inquiries, our political experiences, and our social achievements. But those who leafed through them when they were brand-new, under a bookseller's awning on Rue Mercière in Lyon or Rue Saint-Jacques in Paris – what did they read between the carefully printed lines? Just because the sequence of ideas in these texts confers on them a kind of eternal verity, to our eyes at least, can we conclude that all intellectual attitudes are possible in all periods? Equally possible? A great problem for the history of the human mind.[23]

Febvre proceeds to demonstrate the ways in which Christianity permeated every aspect of men and women's lives in the sixteenth century: from 'birth to death stretched a long chain of ceremonies, traditions, customs, and observances, all of them Christian or Christianized, and they bound a man in spite of himself, held him captive even if he claimed to be free'.[24] Was it possible for any individual, even an 'exceptional man – one of those men, few in number, who show they are capable of being a century ahead of their contemporaries', to challenge religious belief with the mental tools, the *outillage mental,* that were available to him?

Sixteenth-century philosophy, Febvre argues, contained neither the vocabulary nor the syntax to support a serious challenge to religious belief. And the same was true of science, which had neither the tools nor the language to separate the natural from the supernatural. What was missing from the language of philosophy and science invariably set conceptual limits on the 'mental universe' of sixteenth-century man.[25] Febvre emphatically concludes, therefore, that 'no, it would not have been possible for a man like him [Rabelais] to undertake such a thing in a truly serious way. He had not ground on which to stand.'[26] Febvre's argument contains both hermeneutic and structuralist dimensions:

> He argues that man has a need for coherence (vision) in, as well as forms (structures) for, his ideas. In their coherence, prevailing conceptions of the world provide fixed points of orientation against which original ideas must be measured. One reconceives in light of what one already knows. Even when man totally reconceives his world, he must reconcile what he previously believed with his new conceptions. Sixteenth-century man, Febvre contends, no matter how intellectually adventurous, could not totally abandon the religious scheme of thought which was his surest frame of reference.[27]

However, Febvre's conclusion concerning Rabelais continues, 'And his denials could at best have been no more than opinions – paradoxical ways of thinking and feeling that nothing from outside came to the support of or propped up in any real or substantial way, nothing in either the science or philosophy of the time.'[28] This passage suggests that Febvre did not discount the possibility of unbelief, only that it was unimportant: that whatever Rabelais wrote about religion did 'not matter, historically speaking. Because denials that rest solely upon personal impulses and moods are without social significance, without exemplary value, and without any compelling force to those who hear them'.[29] Febvre argued that unbelief could not really engage with Christianity until philosophy and science could successfully separate the natural from the supernatural. In other words, there is an epistemological break, a 'conceptual caesura', between the unbelief of the sixteenth century and the atheism of the eighteenth century. In so doing, Febvre replaced assumptions of evolutionary progress with one of fundamental discontinuities.[30] Febvre, as did Bloch, also reflected the perspective of philosopher Lucien Lévy-Bruhl, comparing the 'primitive mentality' of the sixteenth century to the 'civilized', or rational mentality of the eighteenth.

## ▶ Subsequent generations of *Annales* historians

There is both continuity and change in the direction taken by Bloch's and Febvre's successors in the *Annales* movement. In terms of continuity, *Annales* historians continued to focus upon the centuries before 1789.[31] The most widely admired study by an *Annales* historian in the postwar years, *The Mediterranean and the Mediterranean World in the Age of Philip II* (1949) by Ferdinand Braudel, was the catalyst for one set of changes. The focus of the book is upon the physical environment, the sea and the mountains. Braudel developed a new concept of historical time but – more importantly – people were almost left out altogether. Some critics accused Braudel of geographical determinism, since he attributed man's beliefs and behaviour to the physical environment.[32] Braudel also influenced the direction of the *Annales* movement away from the study of *mentalités* and towards quantitative methods and the statistical analysis of social and economic data.

The return to the preoccupations of Bloch and Febvre came with studies such as Le Roy Ladurie's *Montaillou* (1978). Based upon the detailed records of the Inquisition, investigating a medieval village accused of Cathar heresy, this book revealed peasant men and women's views on, among others things, love, death, work and magic. The study of *mentalités* became more narrowly focused upon specific subjects, rather than cultures as a whole.[33] In many senses these new trends followed Febvre's earlier call for a history of sentiment. But, as we shall see below, one of the criticisms of the plethora of new studies is the absence of any broader theoretical formulation, and this leads us into the criticisms of the *mentalités* approach.[34]

## ▶ Critiques

It is often written of Bloch and Febvre that they never fully 'formulated a theory of mentalities'.[35] There is, in their writings, a lack of analysis 'of the mechanism by which fundamental categories of thought within a given group of social agents become internalized and of unconscious schemata that structure all particular thoughts and actions'.[36] The exception to this criticism is a historian, greatly influenced by the work of Bloch and Febvre, but who was largely independent of the *Annales* circle. [37] Philippe Ariès (1914–84) wrote a history of childhood and the family, *Centuries of Childhood*, published in 1962, which was both influential and controversial.[38] The evidence that childhood and family were conceived quite differently between the medieval period and the eighteenth century led Ariès to consider how the life cycle gradually became identified over this period as a developmental process. His study of childhood is based upon a 'developmental paradigm' that both addresses the theoretical lacunae identified above and seeks to understand the processes of cultural change.[39]

The second critique of *mentalités* is the tendency towards both reification and cultural stasis and the perception of *mentalités* as prisons from which individuals cannot escape, to draw upon Ferdinand Braudel's famous metaphor.[40] This leads to an excessive emphasis upon the degree or extent of cultural or intellectual consensus; both Bloch and Febvre wrote, at times, of '"the medieval Frenchman", or the "sixteenth-century Frenchman" as if there were no important variations in attitude among the inhabitants of France in this period (male and female, rich and poor, literate and illiterate, and so on)'.[41] The degree of consensus implicit within *mentalités* makes it difficult to explain change over time from one system of thought to another, and it has been argued that this is the fundamental problem that all historians of *mentalités* have been unable to answer.[42]

In his wider writings, Bloch clearly believed that material and cultural factors had to be examined in conjunction. Nonetheless, a third critique of *mentalités* is that the original formulation of *mentalités* lacked sufficient attention to economic or social interests. In 1990 the French Marxist historian Michel Vovelle felt compelled to warn against a history of mentalities that detached popular beliefs from their social and economic context, or insisted upon the 'autonomy of the mental universe'.[43] Attention to conflicts of interest are central to understanding change over time, he argued, because 'conflicts of interest make the unconscious conscious and the implicit explicit, and this way they lead to change'.[44]

Bringing conflict to conscious awareness is also central to the second approach to the study of subjectivity and the unconscious to be considered in this chapter. The conflict to which we now turn, however, does not arise out of the economic or social context but is psychological in nature, embedded in the structure of the mind and played out in human development through childhood and youth.

## ▶ Psychoanalysis

Given the nature of the cultural history enterprise to describe, understand, interpret and explain human beliefs and behaviour in the past, it is perhaps surprising that historians have not, on the whole, drawn more upon psychological theories. The exception is psychoanalysis and the ideas of Sigmund Freud and his successors. Psychoanalysis 'burst upon the [historical] profession with a spectacular conjunction of events' in 1958. During that year Erik Erikson published the path-breaking psychoanalytic study *Young Man Luther*; and in the American Historical Association presidential address, the historian William Langer urged historians to include psychoanalytic insights as part of their interpretive practice.[45] Since that time, a number of cultural historians have identified themselves as psycho-historians, using psychoanalytic ideas to explain human beliefs and behaviour in the past. A far larger group of historians have adopted the terminology of the 'unconscious', and other aspects of psychoanalytic theory, without claiming membership of a particular historical school. Psychoanalytic vocabulary became, as historian Keith Thomas pointed out, 'part of ordinary educated discourse'.[46]

Psychoanalysis originated with the work of Sigmund Freud in the late nineteenth century. Along with Karl Marx and Charles Darwin, Freud is one of a triumvirate of thinkers whose theories fundamentally changed the way people in the Western world think about themselves. Freud emphasized the role of instinctual unconscious human drives – sexuality and aggression – at the core of human behaviour, and he argued that these shaped a universal developmental process in the human psyche throughout childhood. The theory emerged out of his work as a doctor treating patients suffering from nervous diseases in late nineteenth-century Vienna, and some historians regard this context as central to understanding the genesis of his ideas.

Freud was born in 1856 in Freiburg, Germany, and studied medicine at the University of Vienna, working first of all in the field of physiology. However, research did not provide adequate income for family life, so Freud set up his own medical practice. He specialized in the treatment of nervous diseases, particularly among wealthy women suffering from the symptoms of hysterical illnesses. The term 'hysteria' came to cover a wide range of symptoms, including 'amnesia, paralysis, unexplained pains, nervous tics, loss of speech, loss of feelings in the limbs, sleep-walking, hallucinations and convulsions.' It was widely believed to be a disease unique to women, the consequence of disorder in the reproductive system. However, the experience treating hysteria led Freud to reject his earlier position on the physiological origins of mental illnesses and he began to seek answers in human psychology instead.[47]

It has been suggested that Freud's turn inward towards the psyche was a response to the obstacles he encountered as a Jew in the increasingly anti-semitic culture of fin-de-siècle Vienna. The failure to achieve academic promotion, in combination with the impact of his father's death, caused Freud to withdraw, both socially and intellectually:

> The more Freud's outer life was mired, however, the more winged his ideas became. He began to detach psychic phenomena from the anatomical moorings in which the science of his day had imbedded them. The speculative daring of his

ideas, such as his theories of the sexual etiology of the neuroses, increased his estrangement from the very men who would have to support his professional advancement. Freud's intellectual originality and professional isolation fed upon each other.[48]

Carl Schorske draws attention to Freud's analysis of his own dreams. The analysis focuses primarily upon his relationship with his father and neglects the broader political or national themes that are also evident.[49] Schorske concludes that Freud constructed 'an a-historical theory of man and society', in order to 'make bearable a political world spun out of orbit and beyond control'.[50]

Over his lifetime Freud published a series of key texts, although he constantly revisited, and sometimes rejected, his earlier conclusions. This is consistent with Freud's characterization of psychoanalysis as 'a *Wissenschaft,* a research programme that included a speculative dimension, and not as a positivistic and predictive science'.[51] *Studies in Hysteria* (1895), written with his friend and colleague Josef Breuer, includes early case histories of patients treated for hysteria. However, Freud's first major psychoanalytic study, *The Interpretation of Dreams,* appeared in 1900. Five years later *Three Essays on the Theory of Sexuality* was published, establishing the centrality of sexual development for psychoanalytic theory and practice. From that point onwards Freud sought to construct a coherent theory, developing the concepts of ego, id and super-ego to explain the structure, and functions, of the human mind.[52]

## ▶ Key concepts

Psychoanalysis is both a theory of individual human psychological development, and a set of therapeutic tools for the treatment of mental neuroses. According to psychoanalytic theory, the developmental process and experiences of infancy and childhood generate unconscious psychological conflicts that are the key determinants of adult human behaviour. Psychoanalysis is therefore a theory of conflict and intense emotions. Freud emphasized the importance of sexual desires that emerge in infancy and conflict with social taboos and controls, resulting in individual neuroses and psychological illnesses. Secondly, psychoanalysis has been described as a 'theory of reading'. Constantly seeking a sub-text, the psychoanalyst looks for the hidden meaning in any statement. Freud's early books, *The Interpretation of Dreams* (1900), *The Psychopathology of Everyday Life* (1901), and *Jokes and their Relation to the Unconscious* (1905), concern the 'deeper meanings of various communications and miscommunications . . . random thoughts, dreams, jokes, slips of the tongue, moments of forgetting'.[53] Finally, psychoanalysis shifts mental neuroses from physical to psychological causes. People fall ill because of their past history; unable to cope with a traumatic incident, individuals suppress conscious recall of the event, only to have it return in the form of psychic conflict later in life. Freud developed a number of key concepts to explain human psychological development; let us turn to look at those ideas that have been most influential among cultural historians.

## ▶ The unconscious

First and foremost among these concepts, and indispensable to psychoanalysis, is that of the unconscious. Freud did not discover or invent the idea of an unconscious mind, but he gave it the pre-eminent role in psychoanalytic theory. The unconscious cannot be located in a particular part of the brain, it can only be inferred from the evidence of thought processes, as Freud suggests in the following passage written in 1915:

> Our right to assume the existence of something mental that is unconscious and to employ that assumption for the purposes of scientific work is disputed in many quarters. To this we can reply that our assumption of the unconscious is *necessary* and *legitimate,* and that we possess numerous proofs of its existence.
>
> It is *necessary* because the data of consciousness have a very large number of gaps in them; both in healthy and in sick people psychical acts often occur which can be explained only by presupposing other acts, of which, nevertheless, consciousness affords no evidence. These not only include parapraxes and dreams in healthy people, and everything described as a psychical symptom or an obsession in the sick; our most personal daily experience acquaints us with ideas that come into our head we do not know from where, and with intellectual conclusions arrived at we do not know how.[54]

The unconscious is central to psychoanalytic theory because it acts as the repository of mankind's instinctual drives, including those problematic desires and needs repressed from consciousness.[55] To deal with these repressed desires, Freud and his colleague Fritz Breuer developed psychoanalytic therapy, which relied upon the 'talking cure' to provide the analyst with insights into the origins of neurotic symptoms lying deep within the unconscious mind. The focus of the theory, and treatment, lay within the 'inner world of the analysand', in his or her relationship with the analyst. Much less attention was paid to the relationship between the individual and their social group or context.[56]

Central to Freud's theory of human psychological development is the Oedipus complex. All human beings, according to Freud, are born with a powerful sexual drive; during the early years of life this is expressed through three developmental

stages, the oral, anal and genital. The experiences of these stages, although different for boys and girls, shape the adult psyche. Expression of these desires may
elicit social disapproval, particularly through the parents, leading to the repression of desire into the unconscious. Freud's approach to male and female sexuality opened the way for a challenge to the wider nineteenth-century cultural beliefs
that linked the biological to the emotional and intellectual, and assigned men and
women fundamentally different characteristics and roles. In *Three Essays on the
Theory of Sexuality* (1905) Freud suggested that the infant's desires were not 'so
much structured along bisexual lines – a struggle between masculine and feminine, or active and passive desires, – as structured by *polysexuality* – the possibility
of having varied desires and objects of those desires'.[57] In other words, in contrast
to nineteenth-century cultural beliefs, there is no biological law determining
heterosexuality. This aspect of psychoanalysis, emphasizing the role of language,
culture and society in shaping instinctual drives into sexual difference and identity, attracted feminist scholars in the 1970s and 1980s because it provided the
basis on which to challenge gendered biological determinism of the 'anatomy is
destiny' variety.[58]

It has been argued that Freud's most significant achievement was the recognition that sexual identity 'emerged from the translation of instinctual drives into
stories' that expressed individual anxieties and fantasies.[59] Central to the Oedipal
conflict is fantasy, or 'phantasy', which is linked to the early days of Freud's treatment of women suffering from nervous diseases, and his attempts to understand
their accounts of parental sexual seductions in childhood. Originally Freud located
the origins of his patients' neuroses in childhood sexual trauma; but later he came
to see these accounts as 'fantasies, emotionally-charged psychic images that served
to represent a cluster of powerful, primitive and often contradictory emotions'.[60]
These fantasies, in other words, were Oedipal in origin and represented wish fulfil-
ment. This aspect of Freud's thought has attracted fierce criticism from those who
argue that it neglects the violence and abuse that is the reality of many children's
lives.[61] While trauma became the focus of subsequent generations of psychoana-
lysts, Freud's transition from actual sexual trauma to the narrator's fantasy, it is
argued, laid the foundation for psychoanalytic theories concerning the role of
unconscious drives in creating psychological conflict.[62]

Freud also identified three different aspects of the human psyche that function
in tension with each other. The id consists of instinctual human desires, powerful
and chaotic. In contrast, the ego is the sense of ourselves as self-conscious beings,
separate from the world around us. It is 'the seat of reason' where 'reality testing,
the making of impartial judgments that distinguish fantasies from actualities by
comparing ideas with perceptions' takes place.[63] Meanwhile the super-ego is the
human conscience, generating guilt and restraining individual behaviour. Freud's

view of human nature was pessimistic and conservative; a change in the economic environment, for example, would not change human nature because of the unruly and irrepressible nature of instinctual human desires.

This pessimism was modified by later schools of psychoanalytic thought that focused more upon the 'adaptive and socially integrative functions of the psyche' – for example, the ego psychology of Anna Freud and Heinz Hartman in the 1930s.[64] During the same period controversy erupted over the psychoanalytic approach taken by Melanie Klein, who placed the mother and weaning at the centre of the child's psychical life. Klein challenged Freud's position that the child's first fantasies emerge in the Oedipal conflict of late infancy. Weaning, according to Klein, represented the first 'major loss, giving rise to a constellation of manically controlling and self-preoccupied persecutory fears and defences'. This experience of early infancy, Klein argued in 1934, 'centrally determines our subsequent psychology'.[65] This approach shifts the psychoanalytic focus away from Freud's concept of 'an unconscious dominated by desire to one permeated with anxiety and the experience of the very young, helpless baby'.[66] Klein's psychoanalytic theories have directly influenced studies of witchcraft, as we shall see later in the chapter.

Psychoanalysis has had a very mixed reception among historians. One criticism concerns the universality of mental processes claimed by psychoanalytic theories. Lucien Febvre, writing in 1925, had little time for a perspective that located man's nature outside history: 'I know that man's essential nature is unchanging through time and space . . . I know that old tune. But that is an assumption, and I might add, a worthless assumption for a historian. For him . . . man does not exist, only men.'[67] Others argue that despite insistence upon a universal process of sexual, psychological development, Freud 'never slighted its possible range of expression or social dimension', a range that covered different times and places.[68] But nonetheless there remains a tension between the universal mental processes and structures central to psychoanalytic theory, and a historicist emphasis upon the constructed and changing nature of human cultural beliefs and behaviour over time.

It is therefore not surprising that psychoanalytic interpretive theory has been applied to very specific areas of cultural history, such as biography, childhood, or sexuality; and group behaviour – such as fascism or the persecution of witches. Let us look at two examples of the use of psychoanalytic theory in historical writing, both from sixteenth-century German history. In the first case, the theory is applied to the life of one individual, the Protestant theologian and reformer Martin Luther. In the second, the subject is community beliefs and behaviour leading to the persecution of witches.

## ▷ The interaction between the psychosexual and the psychosocial

The first exemplar of this approach is the work of Erik Erikson, a practising psycho-analyst described as 'Freud's most direct heir as a psychohistorian'.[69] In *Childhood and Society*, published in 1950, Erikson described the psychoanalytic method as 'essentially a historical method' in its focus upon the individual's past. But his approach differed from that of Freud in a number of respects, particularly in the influence he ascribed to the wider social and cultural context. The intention of this book, Erikson explained, was to 'build a bridge' between the psychosexual and the psychosocial.[70] The bridge Erikson constructed consisted of an eight-stage process of human psychological development, dependent upon critical phases of biological and social growth. The stages move through infancy, childhood, youth, adolescence, adulthood, to old age, and each entails a specific set of psychological and social hurdles for the individual. Erikson's model emphasized 'mutality, adaptive capacities, and learning rather than inherited weaknesses', in contrast to Freud's more pessimistic envisioning of the human mind.[71] The importance of Erikson's paradigm for historians is that it focuses upon the whole of the human life span, not just infancy, and sees later periods of life as equally important for individual psychological development.[72]

Eight years later Erikson published *Young Man Luther*, in which he applied his theory of human development to the life of Martin Luther, the religious leader whose conversion to Protestantism in the sixteenth century led to the Reformation. Erikson's study focused on the first half of Luther's life, that of childhood and youth, despite a paucity of sources. Although the study has been described as a 'pace-setting psychobiography', even admirers acknowledged that 'we cannot be sure that Luther's critical episodes, on which his psychoanalytic biographer has principally drawn, happened in the way they were recorded later, or whether they ever happened at all'.[73] Some of the critical episodes in Luther's life related to his experience of violent beatings, both by his father and later at school, and these are illustrative of Erikson's use of evidence and inference. The following passage, exploring the relationship between Luther's childhood beatings and his later stubborn character, is a good illustration of Erikson's type of psychoanalytic analysis:

> We have also indicated the significance of the choice of the buttocks as the preferred place for corporal punishment: a safe place physiologically, but emotionally potentially dangerous, since punishment aggravates the significance of this general area as a battlefield of parental and infantile wills. The fear that his parents and teachers might ever completely subject him by dominating this area and thus

gaining power over his will may have provided some of the dynamite in that delayed time bomb of Martin's rebellion, and may account for the excessiveness with which Luther, to the end, expressed an almost paranoid defiance, alternating with a depressed conception of himself.[74]

Erikson focuses primarily upon the crisis experienced by Luther during the adolescent stage of psychosocial development, seeking the roots of Luther's adult character and behaviour. The adolescent phase is critical for the development of individual identity, and throughout his life, Erikson argues, Luther experienced a 'protracted identity crisis'.[75] Luther sought to solve the conflicts of his youth, he continues, through taking up the leadership of a new religious movement, one that provided a 'spiritual solution to the conflicts arising from the earlier crises of his psychosocial development'.[76] In this study of Luther, Erikson broadly follows the psychoanalytic paradigm regarding the centrality of childhood experience and unconscious psychological conflict, but his analysis is constructed around a less deterministic and more socially contextualized, and adaptive, theory of psychosocial development. The psychoanalytic model employed by Erikson is premised upon interaction between the experiences of childhood and youth and the historical context.[77] To what extent may similar approaches be found in studies of witchcraft, another field where psychoanalytic approaches have also proved fruitful?

## ▶ Fantasy and the unconscious

British historian Lyndal Roper also found psychoanalytic concepts valuable for the study of witchcraft in Germany during the late sixteenth and early seventeenth centuries. The witchcraft accusations and confessions, Roper suggests, cannot be understood through conventional notions of historical realism and fact. Although witchcraft was a 'fantasy', it was not 'trivial or unreal. Rather it had deep roots in the unconscious'.[78] In her first study, *Oedipus and the Devil*, Roper draws upon the theories of Melanie Klein to understand the 'murderous antagonisms' between women, evident in the witchcraft trials.[79] Roper argues that the persecution of witches was 'pre-Oedipal in content, turning on the relationship to the breast and to the mother in the period before the infant has a sense of sexual identity. The primary emotion of the witchcraft cases, envy, also originates in this early period of life.' In other words, the envy and fear projected by newly delivered mothers on to other women originated in the deep emotions of their own infancy. Fear of childbirth, anxiety concerning the survival of the child, and post-natal depression, she suggests, became focused upon the figure of the lying-in-maid, or wetnurse, if the child began to sicken:

But instead of seeking the source of her ills in post-natal depression, within herself, as we would, the mother's anxieties about the child's fate and her own ability to nourish it were directed outwards, so that harm to either mother or baby was believed to have been caused by another. Here we might make use of what Melanie Klein says about splitting, which allows intolerable feelings of hostility and malice to be projected on to another, so that the mother recognizes only benevolence in herself, projecting the evil feelings about herself on to the 'other' mother.[80]

In her most recent study, *Witch Craze,* Roper also explores the transference and counter-transference in the relationship between the accused and her interrogator. Transference and counter-transference describe the projection of emotion within the therapeutic relationship between analysand and analyst. Freud, Roper suggests, made amused reference to the parallels between his own relationship with hysterical patients and that of the witches' inquisitors, pointing to the emotional participation in the relationship required on both sides. The theory of transference and counter-transference provides a valuable tool for 'understanding how an accused individual and interrogator might together provide a witch "fantasy". . . . In the case of witch interrogations, we are seeing not an attempt at healing, but a collusion with a destructive fantasy which will result in the accused's death.' [81] While Roper rejects a mechanistic or reductive application of psychoanalytic theory to the human psyche at different times and places in the past, she argues that it is impossible for historians to investigate fundamental aspects of 'attachment and conflict' in human life if 'historians declare the effects of primary emotions of this kind to be unknowable . . . because it leaves out of the account the extent to which irrational, deep and unconscious feeling can determine human action'.[82]

## ▶ The limitations of the psychoanalytic approach

Critiques of psychoanalytic interpretations often revolve around their reductive nature and theoretical rigidities. It is interesting to look at the work of the French sociologist Norbert Elias (1897–1990) in this context. Elias drew upon a wide range of approaches, including the use of psychoanalytic concepts, for his innovative and highly regarded study of changing social conduct and manners, and the rise of self-control, in sixteenth-century Europe.[83] The first volume of the study (published in 1939) explores the development of the concept of *civilité*. Elias identified ascending 'thresholds of embarrassment and shame' concerning 'outward bodily propriety', including attitudes towards gestures, clothing, facial expressions, eating, and blowing the nose. The identification of appropriate manners and conduct that entailed a 'stronger restraint on [the] emotions', is linked by Elias to change in the social structure – a 'loosening of the medieval social hierarchy' and the rise of a bourgeois intelligentsia. In this social environment, he argues, it became 'an imperative of tact to observe social differences and to give them unambiguous expression in social conduct'.[84]

Elias deploys the range of psychoanalytic concepts, such as the unconscious, id (often described as the 'drive') and ego, in his study of this 'civilizing process', but he deviates from broader psychoanalytic theory in the emphasis he places upon the individual's social context and relationships. For example, in the early stages of the 'civilizing process', control over uninhibited and spontaneous behaviour is imposed not by parental discipline but by superiors in the social hierarchy:

> Stricter control of impulses and emotions is first imposed by those of high social rank on their social inferiors or, at most, their social equals. It is only comparatively late, when bourgeois classes comprising a large number of social equals have become the upper, ruling, class, that the family becomes the only – or, more exactly, the primary and dominant – institution with the function of installing drive control. Only then does the social dependence of the child on its parents become particularly important as a leverage for the socially required regulation and molding of impulses and emotions.[85]

## ▶ Conclusion

Elias is clear that any research that focuses only upon 'the consciousness of men, their "reason" or "ideas", while disregarding the structure of drives, the direction and form of human affects and passions, can be from the outset of only limited value'.[86] But he suggests that the opposite point of view, one that focuses only on the unconscious and instinctual drives of mankind, is equally flawed because it is reductionist and neglects the individual's wider social relationships and other mental attributes. Furthermore, Elias continues, we cannot have unmediated access to the drives of the id, for 'the libidinal energies which one encounters in any living human being are always already socially processed'. They are, in other words, already modified and manipulated by the ego and super-ego.[87] Elias therefore attributes a central role, contrary to orthodox Freudian theory, to the social context and its influence upon the human psyche – in this case changing sensibility concerning human social conduct. Elias argued, as had Febvre, that historians needed to develop a new 'historical psychology' to investigate the workings of both the conscious and unconscious within specific contexts of human relations.[88]

The appeal for a new 'historical psychology' has remained largely unmet within cultural history. The next chapter will explore the way in which the post-Second

World War cultural Marxists, and historians influenced by symbolic anthropology, increasingly focused upon the role of language in the expression of human subjectivities. Marxist cultural historians certainly did not abandon the link between the worlds of human thought and material reality, but they did redirect attention towards the active, constructive, and creative dimensions of class-consciousness. Following hard upon the heels of cultural Marxists, a younger generation of historians influenced by symbolic anthropology went a step further, focusing almost exclusively upon the figurative and symbolic expression of human consciousness.

# 3 From Agency to Symbols

In the last quarter of the twentieth-century a significant shift took place within cultural history. While always focused primarily upon human subjectivity, cultural historians had nonetheless often linked cultural characteristics or changing *mentalités* to underlying economic or social factors. The degree to which human consciousness was determined by social being, however, began to be questioned more explicitly in the 1960s and 1970s, as historians increasingly gave more weight to the constructive and creative role of human consciousness. A gradual but consistent trend towards the idealist end of the spectrum is reflected in two widely influential approaches to cultural history during these decades. It began with the postwar generation of British Marxist historians, who took Marx's theory of historical **materialism** in new directions. Influenced in particular by their interests in literature and literary theory, Marxist intellectuals such as Raymond Williams and E. P. Thompson rejected simplistic models of economic determinism in favour of an approach to human consciousness that emphasized human agency. The material world of economic deprivation did not disappear in the work of the cultural Marxists, but the new 'history from below' gave an active voice to those at the disadvantaged end of economic relationships. Thompson, for example, emphasized the ways in which customary expectations and religious values were utilized and reframed by the emerging working class to make sense of the changing economic and social relationships of industrializing late eighteenth- and early nineteenth-century Britain.

Roughly a decade after the major impact of Williams and Thompson, a new approach from anthropology shifted the weight of analysis even further towards the figurative and symbolic content of human consciousness. The anthropologist Clifford Geertz's influential book *The Interpretation of Cultures* (1973) based cultural interpretation upon the links between systems of symbolic language and social behaviour. This approach was taken up with enthusiasm by a group of American cultural historians in particular and resulted in innovative interpretive insights into aspects of eighteenth-century French history. Both cultural Marxism and symbolic anthropology can, in retrospect, be seen to be part of a general movement towards the 'linguistic turn' within the humanities, with its focus upon the semiotic dimensions of human culture (the subject of the next chapter). This chapter will explore these earlier developments, beginning with the original formulation of historical materialism by Karl Marx, followed by the decisive intervention of the Italian activist Antonio Gramsci, whose writings emphasized the importance of inherited folklore in shaping proletarian consciousness.

## ▶ Marxism

Karl Marx was born in Trier, Germany, and spent his early adult life in Prussia and France.[1] Many of Marx's ideas about history were developed in the context of revolutionary socialist movements and struggles that culminated in the 1848 Revolution, and the rapid social and economic change of industrialization. Forced to move around under threat from the Prussian authorities, Marx finally settled in England in 1849, where he spent the rest of his life.[2] The theory of history for which he is known is called 'historical materialism', and the basic principles were laid out in *The German Ideology*, written in 1846. According to Marx, the central dynamic in human history is the struggle for physical and material needs: 'life involves before everything else eating and drinking, a habitation, clothing and many other things. The first historical act is thus the production of the means to satisfy these needs, the production of material life itself.'[3] These needs are never satisfied, however, and new needs constantly develop. The ways in which these human material needs are met are, for Marx, the most important influence in human history. The economic arrangements of 'industry and exchange', therefore, formed the base for all other aspects of society. In particular, the interaction between raw materials and human labour created relations of production between people, and these relations rested upon either cooperation or subordination. For Marx, the rest of society – the superstructure of political institutions and legal systems – all derived from the relations of production.

In other words, Marx did not ascribe an independent existence to the realm of human consciousness and ideas, but perceived these as arising out of our material existence, and in particular economic productive relationships. The premises and main ideas of historical materialism are concisely outlined in the following, frequently cited, statement from *Contribution to the Critique of Political Economy* (1859):

> In the social production of their life, men enter into definite relations that are indispensable and independent of their will, relations of production which correspond to a definite stage of development of their material productive forces. The sum total of these relations of production constitutes the economic structure of society, the real foundation, on which rises a legal and political superstructure and

to which correspond definite forms of social consciousness. The mode of production of material life conditions the social, political and intellectual life process in general. It is not the consciousness of men that determines their being, but, on the contrary, their social being that determines their consciousness.[4]

However, every arrangement of productive relations, Marx argued, contained within it contradictions, the seeds of its own downfall. The driving force of social and economic change is human agency: in order to overthrow the dominant class, the subordinate peoples must become aware of their own oppression. Consequently, as Marxist historian Eric Hobsbawm has pointed out, 'the crucial argument about the materialist conception of history has concerned the fundamental relationship between social being and consciousness'.[5] Marx's position on this relationship has often been described as reductionist: that human consciousness corresponds to, and is determined by, the particular economic framework of productive relations. Later Marxists challenged this formulation, and this issue is at the centre of the writings of the Italian communist activist and influential Marxist writer Antonio Gramsci. Writing before the Second World War, Gramsci was to have a profound influence upon subsequent generations of Marxist historians and writers.

## ► Hegemony and the Subaltern

Gramsci was born in 1891 in Sardinia and, despite the imprisonment of his father and consequent impoverishment of the family, won a scholarship to the University of Turin. He studied literature and linguistics, and although forced to abandon his studies through ill-health, these intellectual interests were to influence his subsequent writings as a committed political activist. Leader of the Communist Party of Italy between 1924 and 1926, and an elected parliamentary deputy, he was imprisoned by the fascist regime between 1927 and 1935. In a series of prison notebooks, written under difficult conditions of censorship and smuggled out to Russia after his death, Gramsci embarked on a project to write about a range of topics circling around Italian history and thought.

Many of the topics he wrote about related to literature and culture, and in particular popular literature. Throughout his writings is an unstated political question: 'What are the agencies by which culture is shaped, and to what extent can culture be guided by conscious political agency?'[6] Gramsci believed that the **subaltern** (a term he coined to describe the peasantry and non-elite groups in society) could not become the dominant class by economic and political power alone, but also had to transform cultural beliefs: 'Just as it [the proletariat] has thought to organize itself politically and economically,' he wrote, 'it must also think about organizing itself culturally.' The revolution had to be preceded by a 'new set of standards, a new psychology, new ways of feeling, thinking and living'.[7] As a political activist, Gramsci sought to understand the ways in which old, conservative cultural values could be defeated, and new ideas and consciousness developed in their place, and in the process he made two particular theoretical contributions that were to be picked up by subsequent generations of historians.

Gramsci used the term 'culture' loosely, and rarely addresses the concept directly in his writings. However, in an early newspaper article published in 1917, he defined culture as follows:

> I give culture this meaning: exercise of thought, acquisition of general ideas, habit of connecting causes and effects. For me, everybody is already cultured because everybody thinks, everybody connects causes and effects.[8]

This view of culture is very different from elite notions of culture as art, or literature. Culture here is the everyday understanding of individuals, whether passively or actively acquired, of their human relationships and position in life. Gramsci did not romanticize culture; nor did he see cultures as necessarily bounded, coherent or consistent.[9] In his observations on folklore, which he perceived as a major dimension of subaltern cultural life, he argued that it could not consist of 'elaborated, systematic' conceptions of the world, but was closer to 'a confused agglomerate of fragments of all the conceptions of the world and of life that have succeeded one another in history'.[10] In addition to this complicated, and often unconscious, cultural inheritance, subaltern consciousness was also subject to manipulation by the elite. A folkloric consciousness was inevitably distorted and confused, Gramsci argued, given the dominance of the ruling classes and the subaltern's lack of power.

Gramsci developed the concept of hegemony to describe the complex ways in which the elite, through both coercion and consent, exercised domination over the consciousness of subaltern peoples.[11] The concept of hegemony was a major contribution to Marxist thought in that it drew attention to the interlocking ways – social, political, cultural – in which control over subordinate groups could be maintained. As Raymond Williams, who introduced English-speaking audiences to Gramsci's ideas after the Second World War, later explained:

> Hegemony is then not only the articulate upper level of 'ideology': nor are its forms of control only those ordinarily seen as 'manipulation' or 'indoctrination'. It is a whole body of practices and expectations, over the whole of living: our senses and assignments of energy, our shaping perceptions of ourselves and our world. It is a lived system of meanings and values – constitutive and constituting

– which as they are experienced as practices appear as reciprocally confirming. It thus constitutes a sense of reality for most people in the society. . . . It is, that is to say, in the strongest sense a 'culture', but a culture which has also to be seen as the lived dominance and subordination of particular classes.[12]

However, despite the hegemony of the elite, Gramsci did not abandon belief in the capacity of individuals to consciously develop new and/or critical cultural perspectives. He made a distinction between the passive, uncritical adoption of cultural perceptions and expectations, and a conscious and critical reflexive process of thinking. In a passage on the study of philosophy, Gramsci argued that:

Having first shown that everyone is a philosopher, though in his own way and unconsciously, since even in the slightest manifestation of any intellectual activity whatever, in 'language', there is contained a specific conception of the world, one then moves on to the second level, which is that of awareness and criticism. That is to say, one proceeds to the question – is it better to 'think', without having a critical awareness, in a disjoined and episodic way? . . . Or, on the other hand, is it better to work out consciously and critically one's own conception of the world and thus, in connection with the labours of one's own brain, choose one's sphere of activity, take an active part in the creation of the history of the world, be one's own guide, refusing to accept passively and supinely from outside the moulding of one's personality. . . . The starting-point of critical elaboration is the consciousness of what one really is, and is 'knowing thyself' as a product of the historical process to date which has deposited in you an infinity of traces, without leaving an inventory.[13]

The key features of Gramsci's reflections – the broad definition of culture and its significance for Marxist thought, the concept of hegemony, and the capacity for individual reflexivity – exercised a profound influence over subsequent generations of Marxist theorists and cultural historians. Gramsci fundamentally challenged the idea that cultural beliefs and practices were simply a superstructure, a more or less passive reflection of fundamental economic relationships, as the original Marxist formulation can be taken to imply, and his influence is evident in the much later development of cultural Marxism.

## ▶ Cultural Marxism

Raymond Williams (1921–88), one of the central figures in the development of cultural Marxism in the middle of the twentieth century, also adopted a broad vision of the idea of culture. In a key essay, 'Culture is Ordinary', written in 1958, the personal description of a visit to Hereford cathedral followed by a bus journey home provides the foundation for the subsequent argument that culture is intrinsic to all minds and inseparable from everyday life. In addition, human consciousness and culture are linked to the material context of human production through his meditation on the landscape of the Welsh border country:

> The bus stop was outside the cathedral. I had been looking at the Mappa Mundi, with its rivers out of Paradise, and at the chained library, where a party of clergymen had got in easily, but where I had waited an hour and cajoled a verger before I even saw the chains. . . . The bus arrived, with a driver and a conductress deeply absorbed in each other. We went out of the city, over the old bridge, and on through the orchards and the green meadows and fields red under the plough. Ahead were the Black Mountains, and we climbed among them, watching the steep fields end at the grey wall, beyond which the bracken and heather and whin had not yet been driven back. To the east, along the ridge, stood the line of grey Norman castles; the west, the fortress wall of the mountains. Then, as we still climbed, the rock changed under us. Here, now, was limestone, and the line of the early iron workings along the scarp. The farming valleys, with their scattered white houses, fell away behind. Ahead of us were the narrower valleys: the steel-rolling mill, the gasworks, the grey terraces, the pitheads. The bus stopped, and the driver and conductress got out, still absorbed. They had done this journey so often, and seen all its stages. It is a journey, in fact, that in one form or another we have all made. . . .
>
> Culture is ordinary: that is where we must start. To grow up in that country was to see the shape of culture, and its modes of change. I could stand on the mountains and look north to the farms and the cathedral, or south to the smoke and flare of the blast furnace making a second sunset. To grow up in that family was to see the shaping of minds: the learning of new skills, the shifting of relationships, the emergence of different language and ideas. . . .
>
> Culture is ordinary: that is the first fact. Every human society has its own shape, its own purposes, its own meanings. Every human society expresses these, in institutions, and in arts and learning. The making of a society is the finding of common meanings and directions, and its growth is an active debate and amendment under the pressures of experience, contact and discovery. . . . The growing society is there, yet it is also made and remade in every individual mind. The making of a mind is, first, the slow learning of shapes, purposes, and meanings, so that work, observation and communication are possible. Then, second, but equal in importance, is the testing of these in experience, the making of new observations, comparisons, and meanings. . . . These are the ordinary processes of human societies and human minds, and we see through them the nature of a culture: that it is always both traditional and creative; that it is both the most ordinary common meanings and the finest individual meanings. We use the word culture

in . . . two senses: to mean a whole way of life – the common meaning; to mean the arts and learning – the special processes of discovery and creative effort. Some writers reserve the word for one or other of these senses; I insist on both, and on the significance of their conjunction. The questions I ask about our culture are questions about our general and common purposes, yet also questions about deep personal meanings. Culture is ordinary, in every society and in every mind.[14]

Williams's account of the bus journey from Hereford to Pandy, in the Welsh valley where he grew up, is a metaphor for the making of human consciousness. On this journey, observing everyday human interaction and the changing landscape, Williams touches on many of the key dichotomies of cultural history: for example, elite and everyday, individual and social. But perhaps the first, and most important feature in Williams's journey is the connection between consciousness and culture and the world of production, evoked in the narrative through the powerful images of farm and furnace. His approach to this relationship was later outlined in *Marxism and Literature* (1977), and given the name 'cultural materialism'.[15] In tune with Gramsci, Williams did not propose a deterministic relationship between the material world and that of human consciousness. Rather he emphasized human agency and creativity, and defined determination as both the 'setting of limits *and* the exertion of pressures'.[16] Williams suggests that human consciousness is shaped through an active interaction between inherited ideas and experience, both of which set limits to the process. Williams defines culture, therefore, as a dynamic process in which shared beliefs and behaviours are constantly contested, both at the level of the individual and within society.

Williams' emphasized the intrinsically social nature of all human thought. In particular, and in the context of literary production, he drew attention to the way in which no generation spoke quite the same language. But language alone could not encompass the breadth of social change between generations, which included diverse styles of clothing, architecture, manners, as well as literary 'style'. Williams conceptualized the full range of generational expression (or that of a historical period) as 'structures of feeling'. He acknowledged the difficulty of the term, but explained that the use of the word 'feeling' was intended to convey a much broader concept than that of formal systems of thought, such as **ideology**. It needed to encompass the full range of social attitudes, values, meanings: 'we are talking', he wrote, 'about characteristic elements of impulse, restraint, and tone; specifically affective elements of consciousness and relationships'.[17] Remembering that tension between experience and consciousness is central to Williams's cultural analysis, the concept of structures of feeling was intended by Williams as a tool, a 'cultural hypothesis', through which cultural transformations could be traced and understood.

## ▶ Experience and agency

One criticism of cultural history as a whole has been the failure to adequately explain or identify the processes of cultural change, but in cultural materialism experience and agency remained fundamental to the making (and changing) of human consciousness. These are central, for example, in E. P. Thompson's *The Making of the English Working Class* (1963), a book that widely influenced a generation of historians, including those who might not have described themselves as Marxists. Thompson explored the 'making' of the English working class between 1780 and 1832. Engaging theory and evidence in dialogue, he was determined not to impose a reductive economic model, although this led to criticism by fellow-Marxists.[18] Thompson located the rise of class consciousness within the material context of changing economic and social relationships of production, but this is not the major focus of the book. This is the subjective formation of class-consciousness, which Thompson argued was an 'active process, which owes as much to agency as to conditioning'.[19] Men and women were not passive prisoners of their environment. Rather they were active agents drawing upon popular ideas and traditions, including the 'moral economy' and the 'free-born Englishman', to make sense of their new industrial labouring experiences and to challenge oppressive economic relationships. Thompson disagreed with Williams's definition of culture as a 'whole way of life', suggesting that it did not adequately confront 'problems of power and conflict'. Rather than a 'whole way of life', Thompson suggested, it was 'a way of *struggle*'.[20]

Two key concepts lie at the heart of Thompson's work: 'agency', and 'experience'. What he means by these terms is outlined in a polemic on Marxist theory published in 1978. Thompson was enraged by the work of French Marxist philosopher Louis Althusser, whose approach emphasized the determination of structural forces, including the hegemony of ideology, upon working-class consciousness. Such an approach, Thompson believed, de-historicized the past and removed the active human subject. In contrast, Thompson argued that experience pressed upon consciousness and challenged old ways of thinking:

> Experience walks in without knocking at the door, and announces deaths, crises of subsistence, trench warfare, unemployment, inflation, genocide. People starve: their survivors think in new ways about the market. People are imprisoned: in prison they meditate in new ways about the law. In the face of such general experiences old conceptual systems may crumble and new problematics insist upon their presence.[21]

Thompson argued that human subjectivity is the result of a continuous '*dialogue* between social being and social consciousness'. And that dialogue is the basis for the exercise of human agency – the active making of our own history. Thompson does not define agency, although he circles around the concept at different times. At one stage, addressing Engels on the exercise of human will, Thompson describes 'the crucial ambivalence of our human presence in our own history, part-subjects, part-objects, the voluntary agents of our own involuntary determinations.'[22] Class consciousness, Thompson suggested, was not the product of overdetermined structural forces, but arose in a 'moment of becoming, of alternative possibilities, of ascendant and descendant forces, of opposing (class) definitions and exertions, of "double-tongued" signs', and during those moments men and women actively made their own history.[23]

## ▶ Critiques

Thompson's conceptualization of class consciousness became the locus of criticism, in the 1980s, from both Marxist and feminist historians. Coming from the first of these positions, Perry Anderson made two explicit critiques. First of all, he drew attention to Thompson's failure to define 'agency', and his inconsistent use of the term 'experience'. Focusing here on the second of these criticisms, Anderson pointed out that experience could be either individual or collective consciousness in response to specific events, or an intermediary position between the event and the cognitive response. The variable application of the concept of experience arose, Anderson continued, out of the dual meaning implicit in the term: 'experience' could refer to either the events occurring throughout a life, or the process of learning from those events. Secondly, Anderson reminded us that experience does not determine consciousness, for those who live through the same events often emerge with very different perspectives.[24] Thompson did not pay much attention, for example, to those of the working class for whom the experience of factory labour did not lead to a burning desire for economic and political transformation. Thompson later acknowledged the lack of clarity in his formulation of 'experience', but nonetheless argued that the effects of experience upon human consciousness had to be the trigger for resistance to the hegemony of elite ideologies.[25]

Thompson's formulation of the relationship between experience and consciousness was the subject of further criticism from feminist historians. One of the persistent critiques of *The Making of the English Working Class*, in particular, concerned the marginalization of working-class women as historical actors. From the late 1960s onwards, feminist historians had begun to put women and gender analysis at the centre of cultural enquiry. In terms of Marxist historiography, feminist historians initially sought to add women to existing frameworks and categories, but such an approach only resulted in limited gains. The problem was not the lack of working women in the nineteenth-century working class, for they were to be found both in factories and in the skilled trades such as millinery, lace-making, or tailoring. In a seminal article, Joan Scott argued that the conceptualization of class and working-class politics central to *The Making* was resistant to the incorporation of women's lives and experiences because Thompson had constructed a unitary and gendered representation of class and class consciousness that emphasized its secular, radical and rationalist origins. Relatively few artisan women appear to have participated in the protest movements with these antecedents; in contrast, the religious, utopian and expressive movements that attracted greater numbers of women adherents, such as Owenism or the religious movement led by the prophetess Joanna Southcott, were depicted as 'the crazy strain in working-class discourse'. Why, Scott asked, is class consciousness inherent in the first tradition, but not the second?[26]

Many of Scott's criticisms above are encapsulated in Carolyn Steedman's account of her mother's life, and her own working-class childhood in London during the 1950s, first published in 1986. Histories of working-class life and consciousness, Steedman argued, had excluded the mental life of working-class women, and promulgated the idea that the adult experience of class produces a 'shared and even consciousness'.[27] Steedman asked for a place for stories like hers that did not fit the conventional narratives of working-class history. Her mother's life was infused by a longing for the consumer goods and domestic security she did not have: 'Born into "the old working class", she wanted: a New Look skirt, a timbered country cottage, to marry a prince.'[28] Steedman criticized those approaches to class consciousness that define it as 'a possible set of reactions people might have to discovering the implications of the position they occupy within the realm of production', since this failed to recognize 'the development of class-consciousness (as opposed to its expression) . . . as a *learned* position, learned in childhood, and often through the exigencies of difficult and lonely lives'.[29]

Thompson's articulation of the relationship between experience and the development of working-class consciousness also came under fire from historians influenced by new French poststructuralist theories that emphasized the constitutive role of language in human understanding. Gareth Stedman Jones's study of Chartist language in mid-nineteenth-century England was the first written from this perspective. Consciousness could not, Stedman Jones suggested, reflect experience except through the mediation of language that *a priori* frames and organizes that experience in the human mind.[30] The language employed by Chartists, he argued, drew upon radical populist discourses that long pre-dated the movement itself, and this explains why the movement focused upon suffrage and political rights rather than, for example, immediate relief from distress. In this case earlier discourses framed new situations, demonstrating Stedman Jones's thesis that:

Language disrupts any simple notion of the determination of consciousness by social being because it is itself part of social being. We cannot therefore decode political language to reach a primal and material expression of interest since it is the discursive structure of political language which conceives and defines interest in the first place.[31]

But both earlier and contemporary generations of cultural Marxist historians were dismayed by the new poststructuralist cultural histories that cut language adrift from the material dimensions of culture and gave discourse the determining role in human consciousness. Their concerns were reflected in the wider schism among historians over the implications of poststructuralism that continues to the present.[32]

## ▶ Technological determinism

Before leaving the subject of cultural materialism let us briefly consider another perspective on the capacity of material change to transform human consciousness. Jack Goody, a Marxist anthropologist and historian, studied at Cambridge concurrently with Williams and Thompson.[33] His seminal study of the transformative impact of writing and literacy upon oral societies has more in common with the understanding of historical materialism outlined by the political philosopher Gerald Cohen. Aligning more closely with Marx's original formulation, Cohen defines historical materialism as technological determinism.[34] The mode of communication, Goody suggests, fits within the definition of technology. That is, it 'codified ways of deliberately manipulating the environment to achieve some material objective'.[35] The advent and spread of writing is a 'technology of the intellect', based upon development of scripts, writing materials, and information storage. Furthermore, the new 'interaction between the human mind and the written word' led to changes in aspects of human cognition. Intellectual developments that Goody associates with the acquisition of writing include lists, systems of classification and categorization, administrative records, and tables. These in turn enhanced the capacity to reason sequentially through the formal 'processes of reorganizing information and reviewing an argument'. It is essential, Goody argues, that anthropologists (and historians) recognize the impact of technologies, 'either material or of the intellect', upon the human mind. Historians, however, have focused more upon the ways in which the advent of printing exponentially expanded the impact of writing, enabling major religious and intellectual movements such as the Reformation, and the Scientific Revolution.[36]

## ▶ Symbolic anthropology

In the 1980s, cultural historians became interested in the approaches of symbolic anthropologists, and theories about symbolic language and behaviour became the second major influence moving cultural history in a semiotic direction. Anthropological and historical approaches were traditionally considered largely incompatible due to the structural-functionalism and synchronic dimensions of most anthropological enquiry during the twentieth century. From the founder of the discipline of sociology, Émile Durkheim, anthropologists had adopted a functionalist perspective: an emphasis upon the mechanisms (rituals, ceremonies) that fulfilled the function of social cohesion.[37] Functionalism later became allied with structuralism, defining social institutions and relationships as the means of ensuring the survival and stability of the social system as a whole. Under the influence of structural functionalism the work of British anthropologists became largely **synchronic**, investigating societies at a given point in time. The combination of structural-functionalism and synchronicity did not fit well with conventional historical interest in political and social change over time.

But there were other aspects of anthropological enquiry that seemed far more fruitful for historians. These included the value of taking a holistic approach, looking at societies and cultures as a whole instead of separating out different aspects into discrete areas of study; and the importance of everyday life in anthropological accounts, rather than the traditional historical focus upon the political and public aspects of the past.[38] By the 1980s, a third dimension had also come to the fore, that of new ways of understanding and interpreting symbolic behaviour.[39] All these dimensions of anthropological enquiry were to be found in the theoretical approach of American anthropologist Clifford Geertz (1926–2006), who exercised considerable influence over a generation of cultural historians.

## ▶ Thick description

From the 1970s onwards Clifford Geertz was the foremost anthropologist in the field of symbolic anthropology. Taught at university by the structural-functionalist sociologist Talcott Parsons, he had been influenced by the latter's conceptualization of culture as a 'level of abstraction' of social relations. Talcott Parsons constructed his analysis of society around three levels: a 'cultural system' of **symbols** and meanings; a 'social system' of norms and institutions, and a 'personality system', comprised of a system of motivations.[40] The idea of interrelated systems was central to the approach Geertz subsequently developed.

Geertz defined culture as a system of symbols and meanings. 'The culture concept to which I adhere', Geertz wrote, '. . . denotes an historically transmitted pattern of meanings embodied in symbols, a system of inherited conceptions expressed in symbolic forms by means of which men communicate, perpetuate, and develop their knowledge about and attitudes towards life.'[41] This was phrased more memorably in the following oft-quoted statement: 'Believing, with Max Weber, that man is an animal suspended in webs of significance he himself has spun, I take culture to be those webs, and the analysis of it to be therefore . . . an interpretive one in search of meaning.'[42] Geertz argued that the anthropologists' goal was to gain access to the symbolic, conceptual world of their subjects in order to be able to 'converse with them'.[43]

The social sciences' failure to develop a theory of symbolic behaviour and figurative language, according to Geertz, left a substantial lacuna in their understanding of 'how metaphor, analogy, irony, ambiguity, pun, paradox, hyperbole, rhythm, and all the other elements of what we lamely call "style" operate'.[44] Geertz's cultural webs were 'encoded in symbolic forms (language, artifacts, etiquette, rituals, calendars, and so on) that were best understood through acts of interpretation analogous to the work of literary critics'.[45] In order to understand the symbolic systems of other cultures, he borrowed a method from the philosopher Gilbert Ryle called 'thick description'. Based upon the premise that human communication is complex and may contain a multiplicity of possible meanings, Geertz argued that an ethnographer's observations of human behaviour had to be contexualized within an account of 'the intentions, expectations, circumstances, settings, and purposes that give actions their meaning'.[46]

How does Geertz's approach to the analysis of cultural expression relate to fundamental questions within cultural history: the assumption of cultural cohesion and the possibility of individual agency? Turning to the first question, Geertz argued that cultural systems had to demonstrate a minimal degree of coherence to justify the label. He noted that although his ethnographies had usually found much more than minimal cultural coherence, he did not believe that coherence in itself should be the major criterion by which to judge the validity of cultural description.[47] To what extent, then, did he believe individuals could exercise agency? **Thick description** explicitly includes the intentions and purposes of historical actors and since Geertz insists that culture is understood from the perspective of the participants, it could be said to incorporate a powerful sense of agency.[48] Nonetheless, he emphasized that the individual only acts within socially established frameworks of meaning, and his or her focus is upon understanding a cohesive symbolic system, not a contested or fragmented culture.[49]

The tightly woven symbolic world invoked by Geertz may owe a great deal to his theory relating to the origins of culture, which draws an analogy between cultural patterning and genetic programming.[50] In 'The Growth of Culture and the Evolution of Mind' Geertz argues that the human brain and culture evolved together and remain organically linked.[51] In this way, it has been argued, Geertz 'transcends the material/ideal dichotomy . . . by a substantial, scientifically-based account of the inescapable complementarity of "material" and "ideal" in the human condition'.[52] There are two consequences of this position. First of all, it places biological and linguistic structures on the same level:

> If Geertz is right, as I firmly believe he is, semiotic systems are not unworldly or ghostly or imaginary; they are as integral to the life of our species as respiration, digestion, or reproduction. Materialists, this suggests, should stop worrying and love the symbol.[53]

However, the symbolic cultural theory Geertz builds upon this **ontological** foundation proposes a very close fit between the social and the symbolic worlds. There is little space in this circular relationship that permits conflicting or multiple representations of reality.

Geertz demonstrated his approach in a detailed study of a cockfight in a Balinese village in 1958.[54] The description includes a great deal about the psychological identification of Balinese men with their cocks (noting that the double meaning here works in both English and Balinese), and the large sums of money gambled on the outcome. He concluded that the cockfights reflect and dramatize conflicts and status concerns within the community, enabling dangerous rivalries and hostilities to be enacted in the form of play:

> Drawing on almost every level of Balinese experience, it brings together themes – animal savagery, male narcissism, opponent gambling, status rivalry, mass excitement, blood sacrifice – whose main connection is their involvement with rage and the fear of rage, and, binding them into a set of rules which at once contains them and allows them play, builds a symbolic structure in which, over and over again, the reality of their inner affiliation can be intelligibly felt.[55]

Critics argued that Geertz did not adequately consider the real social and economic consequences of the cockfight, given the enormous sums won or lost.[56] This lacuna may be one consequence of the synchronic nature of the study, which neglected the long-term effects of the cockfights. Anthropologists have commented upon Geertz's apparent neglect of relationships of power and domination.[57]

## ▶ Symbolic behaviour and figurative language

In what ways did symbolic anthropology influence cultural history in the latter decades of the twentieth century? Let us look at two of the best examples of symbolic cultural analysis, both published in 1984: *The Great Cat Massacre* by Robert Darnton, and Lynn Hunt's, *Politics, Culture and Class in the French Revolution*. Acknowledging his intellectual debt to Geertz, Robert Darnton describes his study as part of both 'l'histoire des mentalités' and 'history in the ethnographic grain'. Darnton explores an incident in Paris in the late 1730s, in which cats were massacred by printing apprentices. His source is an account written some thirty years after the event by one of the participants. The author described the massacre of the cats as one of the funniest events of his career, and Darnton suggests that 'by getting the joke of the great cat massacre, it may be possible to "get" a basic ingredient of artisanal culture under the Old Regime.'[58] This is a similar approach to that of Geertz: both the cockfight and the cat massacre are symbolic vehicles through which to interpret the wider culture.

All aspects of the story are subject to the detailed contextual analysis of 'thick description', from the ceremonial cycles of the carnival, when the conventional rules of behaviour were turned upside down, to the symbolic significance of cats in French culture. The torturing of cats, Darnton suggests, may be found in a wide range of French rituals over the course of the ceremonial year. Certain symbolic meanings were attached to many animals, but particularly to cats. Associated with witchcraft, occult powers and sex, cats were also identified with the master or mistress of the house:

> Witchcraft, orgy, cuckoldry, charivari, and massacre, the men of the Old Regime could hear a great deal in the wail of a cat. What the men of the rue Saint-Séverin actually heard is impossible to say. One can only assert that cats bore enormous symbolic weight in the folklore of France and that the lore was rich, ancient, and widespread enough to have penetrated the printing shop.[59]

The apprentices, resentful and angry at their poor treatment, Darnton concludes, vented their anger in the only way they could – symbolically through the massacre of the cats. The apprentices found the incident funny because it was the only way to 'turn the tables' on their master:

> they used the massacre to put him symbolically on trial for unjust management of the shop. They also used it as a witch hunt, which provided an excuse to kill his wife's familiar [*la grise*, her *chatte favorite*] and to insinuate that she herself was the witch. Finally, they transformed it into a charivari, which served as a means to insult her sexually while mocking him as a cuckold. . . . The men subjected his wife to symbolic aggression of the most intimate kind, but he did not get it. . . . .
>
> The joke worked so well because the workers played so skillfully with a repertory of ceremonies and symbols.[60]

Darnton's account of the cat massacre, and his use of symbolic analysis, attracted considerable debate.[61] One critique drew attention to two problems with Darnton's analysis. First of all, the existence of a paradox in the construction of a complex symbolic analysis based upon a straightforward reading of the original account, treating it as a transparent reflection of reality. In other words, should not Darnton have considered the **narrative** and linguistic functions of the original text? Secondly, the relationship between symbols and that which they purport to represent is far more unstable and problematic than Darnton's account allows. The hierarchies and distinctions within French society, and wide variety of contexts within which symbolic forms were expressed, makes questionable the assumption that these were uniformly shared and understood.[62] Historians argued that *The Great Cat Massacre* is 'overdetermined' in the sense of a hermeneutically coherent narrative, leaving little room for contestation or alternative readings.[63]

The criticism of *The Great Cat Massacre* raised the unresolved problem concerning ways to assess the validity of symbolic interpretation. Although Geertz argued that it should, in principle, be possible to assess the conceptual framework of a cultural interpretation as for a scientific experiment, he did not believe the means to do so existed at that time.[64] Ultimately, he concluded, cultural analysis of this kind was 'guessing at meanings, assessing the guesses, and drawing explanatory conclusions from the better guesses'.[65] While Darnton accepted that symbols could have different meanings at the same time, nonetheless he argued that there were constraints on interpretation, since they 'draw on fixed patterns of behavior and an established range of meanings. The historian can explore that range and map it with some precision, even if he cannot know precisely how everyone made use of it.'[66]

In a very different kind of approach, Lynn Hunt's analysis of the French Revolution, published in 1984, explicitly aimed to revitalize revolutionary politics through a study not of political history, but of the values and expectations – the political culture – that gave the French Revolution coherence and unity. Hunt rejected previous approaches that explained the revolutionary political culture in relation to social structures or social identity. Political culture, she argued, could best be understood through symbolic practices, including types of rhetoric and the adoption of particular symbols and rituals. With reference to Geertz, she suggested that 'the exercise of power always requires symbolic practices. There is no government without rituals and without symbols. . . . In a sense, legitimacy is the general agreement on signs and symbols.'[67]

An example of her approach may be found in the first section of the book, on the 'Poetics of Power'. During the revolution 'words came in torrents', and 'were invested with great passion' in all aspects of social life. For example, words linked to the *Ancien Régime* were replaced by new names. Lawyers wishing to continue to practise relinquished roles as *Procureurs* and *Avocats* in favour of the simple title *hommes de loi*. More significantly, the revolutionary oath underlined the speaker's identification with the revolution, and 'the ritual use of words' became a 'replacement for the charisma of kingship'. To understand the changing forms of expression during the revolution, Hunt turns her attention to its rhetorical and persuasive dimensions. For example, the revolutionaries rejected patriarchal models of authority for their seals and rituals, and drew upon feminine classical allegories in which the father was always absent. The revolutionaries, Hunt suggests, were 'rhetorically killing the king, their father, long before the Convention actually voted the death sentence'.[68]

One consistent criticism of cultural history has been the inability to explain cultural change. Revolution, of course, is a fulcrum of rapid and intense change. Hunt rejected previous analyses of the French Revolution that placed it within conventional causal explanations of historical development that prioritized the roles of economic and social structures. These were changed very little by the revolution she suggests; the changes that took place were in the realm of politics, and it is 'the emergence of the political culture of revolution' that requires explanation.[69] While accepting that the structural failings of the *Ancien Régime* and division among the elites opened up the space for competing political forms, she argues that the new political culture that emerged during the revolution was actively shaped by rhetoric and symbolism. In this argument, language and symbolic forms of thought actively influence the course of history, and are not simple reflections of pre-existing social or economic structures. The new political language, images and rituals appealed primarily to those on the periphery: rural rather than urban, south not north, and the younger generation. The question that remains is: why did the rhetoric and symbolism of revolutionary politics, originating as they did from within classical and Enlightenment thought, resonate so strongly with those on the margins?

## ▶ Conclusion

While both cultural Marxism and symbolic anthropology retain a relationship between material reality and human consciousness, they reject a reductionist interpretation in which the former determines the latter. In both these approaches to cultural history the constructive and creative elements of human consciousness are given a role at least equal to that of economic and social factors in shaping human history. However, on the question of cultural change, the two approaches differ significantly. Marxism is a model of economic and social transformation, into which cultural Marxists injected the capacity for active, conscious agency by historical actors. Relationships of power and conflict are central to this approach, and experience, despite its conceptual difficulties, remains the catalyst for changing class consciousness. In contrast, Geertz's theory – the symbolic mediation of reality by historical actors – is circular and synchronic. Its strengths lie in revealing the depth and complexities of cultural systems, but it is inadequate to explain cultural change. To do this, historians must modify Geertz's approach, looking for diversity as well as cohesion, including conflicting and contested symbolic meanings – from which changing cultural perspectives may emerge – and to the **diachronic**, as well as the synchronic, dimensions of human societies and cultures.

In this context, the work of the French sociologist Pierre Bourdieu (1930–2002) is potentially instructive, and pulls together the themes of this chapter. His conceptual framework appears fruitful for cultural historians wrestling with these issues but anthropologists and sociologists have so far proved to be more receptive. Dissatisfied with the limitations of a symbolic approach, cultural analysts began to look for a new framework that would encompass a less unified and static conceptualization of culture, one that encompassed its fractures, power relations, contradictions and changes. Bourdieu's understanding of 'culture' as a performative term addressed precisely these issues: culture as 'practice', rather than a learned set of rules and meanings, and in particular a practice permeated with miscommunication and therefore requiring constant improvisation and adaptation. Bourdieu had been greatly influenced, while working at the University of Pennsylvania in the 1960s, by the work of the sociologist Erving Goffman. Goffman's original approach to social interaction was developed in *The Presentation of Self in Everyday Life* (1959), in which he analysed everyday human interaction and behaviour as complex drama.[70] Adopting the metaphor of a game, rather than that of the theatre, Bourdieu emphasizes the performative, dynamic and strategic aspects of social and cultural behaviour.

It has been argued that Bourdieu proposes, as did Goffman, that individuals are neither autonomous nor entirely socially determined. However, Bourdieu's approach to the shaping of human consciousness gives a powerfully self-replicating role to social structures such as the family, or social class. Bourdieu introduced the term 'habitus' to explain the ways in which individuals are able to participate in social games. A difficult concept, 'habitus' includes all the forms of collective socialization from childhood onwards, for example, within the family and through the education system, resulting in 'systems of durable, transposable *dispositions*'.[71] Another way of defining 'habitus' is as an 'embodied sensibility that makes possible structured improvisation'.[72] As this suggests, dispositions are more than just cultural and social rules, and include a wider sense of the whole 'game' that enables individuals to adapt and improvise. Nonetheless, they do so within social structures such as social class, or the family, and it remains difficult to see how social or cultural transformations might occur under this model.[73] Bourdieu's theorization, sometimes described as post-Marxist, remained closely embedded in empirical research that acknowledged the existence of a real social world and economic power. In this sense, Bourdieu, while acknowledging the role of mental schemas in shaping human consciousness, differs from the semiotic theorists of the next chapter.

# 4 Semiotics and Discourse

During the 1980s and 1990s historians in general were engulfed by an often-acrimonious debate over theoretical developments that were known collectively as 'the linguistic turn'. The new approaches entailed a fundamental shift in theoretical perspective, and ultimately reconfigured traditional areas of enquiry such as the history of medicine and colonial history. The 'linguistic turn' encapsulates a major change in emphasis within historical explanation, one that gives language the starring role in the creation of historical meaning. This posed a direct challenge to the core principles of empirical epistemology that had formed the bedrock of historical research for over a century: the rigorous examination and knowledge of historical evidence, verified by references; impartial research, devoid of prior beliefs and prejudices; and an inductive method of reasoning, from the particular to the general. Implicit within these principles is a specific theory of knowledge that was to be fundamentally challenged by the 'linguistic turn'. First of all, the past exists independently of the individual's mind, and is both observable and verifiable. Secondly, through adherence to the research principles above, the historian is able to represent the past objectively and accurately. In other words, the truth of an historical account rests upon its correspondence to the facts. While many historians doubted that objective truth could ever be fully attained, most were reluctant to abandon that as a goal.[1]

In contrast, cultural historians since the nineteenth century had provided a parallel stream within historiography that emphasized the interpretive, subjective and provisional nature of historical representation. Burckhardt and Dilthey, for example, drew attention to the essential role played by the historian's own consciousness in the construction of accounts of the past. While Dilthey retained the desire to achieve a scientific credibility for the practice of hermeneutics, he nonetheless acknowledged that it was impossible to efface the perspective of the observer or interpreter. Both historians emphasized the role of 'intuition' (in Burckhardt's case) or understanding and interpretation (in Dilthey's). Cultural historians have also always paid close attention to language and meaning: one thinks, for example, of Dilthey's struggle to develop a robust form of hermeneutics, or the emphasis upon the figurative and symbolic nature of human expression among historians influenced by anthropology and literary theory. Since the time of Burckhardt, cultural historians have used the terminology of 'representation', rather than that of historical 'reconstruction', and were far more receptive to the 'linguistic turn'. It is not surprising, therefore, that the shift in historical consciousness at the end of the twentieth century is also described at times as 'the cultural turn'.

## ▶ Key transformative influences

A number of intellectual currents within historical scholarship contributed to the 'linguistic turn' during the last decades of the twentieth century. Gender theory was one of the most important transformative influences. A generation of feminist historians, seeking to understand the subordinate and unequal position of women, rejected the biological essentialism that ascribed social roles to sexual and reproductive differences. A new concept, that of **gender**, separated the biological categorization of sex from the social and cultural roles assigned to men and women at different times and in different places.[2] Feminist historians were, therefore, among the first to understand the power of social discourses to frame and constrain biological difference.[3] The explosion of gender history, beginning in the 1970s, followed a trajectory that ultimately encompassed both psychoanalytic perspectives and poststructuralism.[4] We will pick up the implications of poststructuralism for gender and cultural history again a little later in the chapter.

A second challenge to objective **empiricism** came with the publication of Hayden White's book *Metahistory* in 1973.[5] 'No one writing in this country at the present time has done more to wake historians from their dogmatic slumber,' wrote Dominick LaCapra a decade later.[6] White utilized tools within existing literary theory to mount a challenge to objective empiricism, arguing (in an earlier essay published in 1966) that historians were disingenuous to claim that their work 'depend[ed] as much upon intuitive as upon analytical methods', while their professional training focused almost entirely upon the latter.[7] Historians had lost sight, he argued, of the value of the 'historical imagination' for understanding the human condition. To demonstrate his point, *Metahistory*, published seven years later, explored the narrative modes of four leading nineteenth-century European historians: Michelet, von Ranke, Tocqueville and Burckhardt; and four philosophers of history: Hegel, Marx, Nietzsche and Croce, to demonstrate the value of 'historical imagination' during 'history's golden age'.[8]

White argued that language, and linguistic protocols, fundamentally shape historical narratives. They do so through the theoretical concepts and narrative structures historians use to construct their accounts of the past. In addition, he suggested, historians 'prefigure their field of study' in a linguistic paradigm that fundamentally determines the story that they write:

> Histories combine a certain amount of 'data', theoretical concepts for explaining these data, and a narrative structure for their presentation.... In addition, I maintain, they contain a deep structural content which is generally poetic, and specifically linguistic in nature, and which serves as the precritically accepted paradigm of what a distinctively 'historical' explanation should be. This paradigm functions as the 'metahistorical' element in all historical works that are more comprehensive in scope than the monograph or archival report.[9]

The 'metahistorical' element of historical writing, White argued, is present right at the start when the historian begins to think about his or her subject, framing it as 'an object of mental perception' through the medium of linguistic **tropes**.

Tropes are the underlying linguistic structures of poetic or figurative language. White maintains that historians are constrained by these linguistic structures, identifying four tropes that shape the 'deep structural forms of the historical imagination': metaphor, metonymy, synecdoche and irony.[10] For example, Burckhardt's history of the Renaissance is framed by irony, for it 'abandons the epic mode in favour of an ironic stance and produces a theory of history that is . . . both an accurate prediction of the rise of the future and a symptom of the illness that will bring it into being'.[11] White concludes that tropes shape the narrative emplotment, argument and ideology deployed by historians in their accounts of the past. But what causes a historian to employ a particular trope? White provides no explanation of how these choices are made, and critics have asked, 'since history cannot begin with documents (the process is already well under way before a document is confronted), what is at the bottom of White's system? Where is its *beginning*?'[12] The limited range of permissible representational forms identified by White may also contribute to the resistance among historians to his ideas.[13]

White's critique derived from well-established literary theory, and while profoundly influential in raising questions about the construction of historical narrative, it should not be perceived as synonymous with the linguistic turn. There are similarities: for example, both literary theory and the linguistic turn emphasize that language is not a transparent medium that simply reflects an external reality. But there is also an important difference. Literary theory helps historians to understand the complex construction of texts, but it is not required to consider epistemological questions central to historical enquiry, such as the relationship between representation and reality.[14]

Questions about the construction of gender roles, and the influence of tropes within historical narrative, were two 'detonators' that shook the foundations of empirical historical methodology, and prepared the ground for poststructuralist linguistic theories that put the relationship between language and reality at the centre of enquiry. Although poststructuralist theories came to influence historians only towards the end of the twentieth century, they are based upon a linguistic model constructed much earlier. Saussurian structural linguistics, to which we now turn, posits that language determines human consciousness and that nothing arrives in human consciousness that has not already been linguistically precoded.[15] The inheritors (and modifiers) of Saussure's original linguistic structuralism have driven the 'linguistic turn' of the past three decades.

## ▶ Linguistic structuralism

Linguistic structuralism originated in the study of languages, and the attempt 'to uncover the internal relationships which give different languages . . . their form and function'.[16] The key figure is Swiss linguist Ferdinand de Saussure (1857–1913), who taught at the University of Geneva between 1891 and 1913. The conceptual approach for which Saussure is known, structural linguistics, is outlined in *Cours de linguistique générale*, published in 1916. In practice, the *Cours* was compiled by Saussure's students from their lecture notes after his death, and published later under his name.[17] The *Cours* established the principles of general linguistics – the study of how a language works (in contrast to historical linguistics, the history and development of a language over time). And although received with some praise, Saussure's ideas did not have a significant impact among English language scholars until the *Cours* was translated into English in 1959.[18]

Over the course of the twentieth century, language 'has passed from being the transparent, presumedly indifferent medium of thought to being a central and intractable problem of philosophy. We have become aware that what we think is conditional on the structure of the language in which we think.'[19] Saussure is one of the key thinkers in this shift of perspective, and his approach revolved around the word as a linguistic sign (he was less interested in the grammatical structures of language). This way of thinking about language has a long heritage, dating back at least to Aristotle and Plato, and the use of the term 'signs', rather than 'words', emphasizes the 'signifying function – the mechanics of meaning and interpretation'.[20] However, only when the study of signs extended beyond philosophy did this approach acquire the title of **semiology**, or semiotics. Saussure and the American polymath Charles Sanders Pierce are generally regarded as the founders of the modern semiology, or the 'science of signs'.[21]

Two features of Saussure's theory should be noted here. First of all, he studied language synchronically, capturing it at a particular moment in time. The term he used, *état de langue*, described the 'snapshot picture that we get of any language at a particular stage of its development'.[22] Secondly, he made a distinction between *langue,* the language system or structure, and *parole,* speech or individual utterances. *Langue* is 'the "system" or totality of language stored in the "collective consciousness"', whereas *parole* is the 'actual utterance, in speech or writing'. This bifurcation of language into two components reminds us of the distinction between the collective and the individual within structuralism, and the priority it assigns to the former.[23]

Saussure's linguistic explanation consists primarily of three important elements: the unity of the sign, its autonomy from reality, and a differential – rather than referential – foundation for meaning. Signs consist of two inseparable dimensions: the *signifier* is the phonetic or acoustic aspect of the sign, and the *signified* the semantic or conceptual aspect. The linguistic sign is arbitrary, with no deterministic relationship to the object, or *referent*, to use Saussure's term, that it describes. The arbitrary nature of the sign is significant, because it indicates that language is not to be understood as synonymous with reality.[24] Had Saussure stopped at this point he might only be remembered for reviving a 'venerable perspective on language' submerged by the nineteenth-century emphasis upon historical linguistics. But he added a further, original aspect to the study of the linguistic sign: that 'each signifier and signified consists of nothing but *difference* from every other signifier and signified in the system': 'every sign', Saussure wrote, 'rests purely on a negative co-status'.[25] In other words, the meaning of the sign is determined internally by its relationship of difference to other signs within the language, characteristically as binary oppositions.

Two immediate problems in Saussure's linguistic theory present themselves for historians. The first is the question of historical change in conceptual thought. Saussure's approach was resolutely synchronic; his model does not accommodate change and therefore rests upon a view of society as essentially conflict-free. Secondly, the individual human subject disappears entirely, 'reduced to the function of an impersonal structure'.[26] The emphasis upon *langue* rather than *parole*, upon the formal structure of language rather than its everyday manifestation in speech, negates the possibility of human agency, since it 'privileges the hidden, unconscious operation of synchronic structures over conscious, purposive individual activity'.[27]

## ▶ Language as dialogic heteroglossia

It is interesting to compare an alternative model of language by a critic of Saussure, the Russian philosopher and literary theorist Mikhail Bakhtin (1895–1975). Bakhtin, whose writings were only discovered by the West at the end of the 1960s, rejected the abstraction of linguistic structuralism and argued that language should be understood within the social context, and as the product of verbal interaction. Growing up in Vilnius and Odessa, cities with diverse populations with a wide variety of languages and cultures, undoubtedly contributed to Bakhtin's perception of language as 'multiplicity and diversity of voices . . . a "dialogized heteroglossia"'.[28] Language is fundamentally 'dialogic', Bakhtin argued; that is, it could only be understood when viewed as relational and socially contexualized within 'the chain of speech communication'.[29]

Bakhtin's approach to language diverged from that of Saussure in a number of significant ways, and influenced later generations of postcolonial scholars in particular. First of all the concept of a 'dialogized **heteroglossia**' encompasses a diversity of perspectives and conflicting interests, making language the focus of conflict and therefore change. In particular, Bakhtin identified the boundaries between cultures as the site where the most creative cultural understandings could emerge.[30] Secondly, his linguistic theory provided the foundation for a materialist theory of consciousness, since 'human consciousness was the subject's active, material, semiotic intercourse with others, not some sealed interior realm divorced from these relations'.[31]

## ▶ The influence of linguistic structuralism and semiotics

The influence of structural linguistics and semiotics upon cultural history has been profound over the past three decades. Saussure's writings on the science of signs were, however, 'scattered and fragmentary' and only appeared in print gradually over an extended period. Consequently the ideas of linguistic structuralism reached cultural historians through a variety of routes.[32] Two in particular stand out: in the work of the French anthropologist Claude Lévi-Strauss, and through the writings of the French poststructuralist philosophers and theorists Michel Foucault and Jacques Derrida.

Lévi-Strauss is possibly the most influential anthropologist of the twentieth century, and certainly the one most deeply influenced by structuralism. While in New York during the Second World War he was introduced to linguistics and linguistic analysis by Roman Jakobson, and his subsequent research project and method owed a great deal to Saussure.[33] Just as Saussure 'expelled individual practices and diachrony [change over time] from the field of linguistics', Lévi-Strauss focused upon social life as a system, 'a set of relations that precede the individual'. He was not interested in 'indigenous conceptions', since these, he argued, could not explain the 'underlying reality'.[34] It has been suggested that social anthropology was particularly receptive to structuralist ideas for three reasons: first of all, the fact that both the study of different societies and that of different languages will lead to the discovery of similarities and differences; secondly, the existing dominance of the synchronic approach in anthropology; and finally, the already established functionalist perspective within the discipline, in which each part plays a particular role in relationship to the whole.[35]

Lévi-Strauss emphasized the primacy of the mind over the social: the various aspects of culture – kinship, exchange, marriage – are 'symbolic systems'. We must never, he wrote, 'lose sight of the fact that, in both anthropological and linguistic research, we are dealing strictly with symbolism'.[36] Lévi-Strauss applied the tenets of linguistic structuralism, in which dichotomous thinking or binary oppositions are embedded within human language, to the study of cultures and myths. For example, the myths of the Bororo Indians of central Brazil and those of surrounding indigenous peoples are understood in terms of binary oppositions, between fire and water, or the fresh and the decayed. 'The function of signs', he wrote in the introduction, 'is, precisely, to express the one by means of the other. . . . I have always aimed at drawing up an inventory of mental patterns.'[37] There is no doubt that binary concepts permeate both language and historical writing, and it is very difficult to avoid them. Many of the theoretical debates within cultural history pivot around binary oppositions, such as self/other, individual/collective, subjective/objective, ideal/material, or synchronic/diachronic. But is dichotomous thinking necessarily as inflexible as it appears within structuralism?

One critique draws attention to the complexity of potential meanings within binary oppositions, and their instability over time. Social anthropologist and cultural historian Jack Goody challenges both the dichotomous and synchronic dimensions of Lévi-Strauss's structuralism. No 'stationary, frozen system' of binary formulations based upon polarities and analogies such as right/left; light/dark; white/black; man/woman, Goody suggests, can possibly accommodate the 'ambiguity and contradiction [that] lie close to the heart of the communicative and cognitive processes'.[38] However, he is also unconvinced by later poststructuralist attempts to deconstruct and replace binary oppositions. Rather than being rejected, he argues, binary oppositions need to be approached historically and contextually. For instance, taking an example from his research, social attitudes towards flowers change – societies may be 'floriphobe' or 'floriphile' at different times in their history.[39]

The rigidities of linguistic structuralism were increasingly challenged within French intellectual circles associated with the literary theory journal *Tel quel* from 1960 onwards, culminating in a movement described as 'poststructuralism'. The term 'post' should not be taken as a rejection of all aspects of structuralism, but more as a critique and development from within. The centrality of language as constitutive of human subjectivity remained at the core of poststructuralist thinking, and structuralist ideas continued to form the basis of poststructuralist methods such as discourse analysis. However, Saussure's aspirations to establish a scientific interpretive model were rejected by the new theorists. For the prac-

tice of cultural history, it was the poststructuralist approaches of French philosophers Michel Foucault and Jacques Derrida that were to have the most profound
influence.

## ► Michel Foucault (1926–84)

The French theorist through whom many English-language historians first became
aware of language's structuring dimension was Michel Foucault. It may seem
slightly inappropriate to begin with a brief survey of Foucault's life history since
he rejected the notion that a text could be understood by reference to an individual author. Nonetheless, on occasions Foucault commented on the influence
personal experience exercised upon the subjects he had chosen to investigate, and
we will return to this point again in the context of postcolonial cultural history.[40]
Born in Poitiers in 1926, Foucault grew up in a wealthy professional middle-class
family. He was educated in Paris at 'one of the most prestigious schools in France',
before entering the École Normale Supérieure to study psychology and philosophy.[41] In 1961 he completed his doctorate on the subject of madness and reason,
publishing it as *Madness and Civilisation*, followed later by *The Birth of the Clinic* in
1963. After a spell teaching in Tunisia, he became head of Philosophy at
Vincennes, followed by a Chair in the History of Systems of Thought at the Collège
de France in 1970. Major works published during this period include *The
Archaeology of Knowledge* in 1969; *Discipline and Punish* in 1975; and the first
volume of *History of Sexuality* in 1976. During the decades of the 1960s and 1970s,
widespread political and social movements – anti-war, anti-racist, feminist –
critiqued and actively challenged political regimes across the world. It was in the
context of this social and cultural ferment that Foucault developed his particular
analytical approach to human subjectivity.

Foucault's body of work is, however, difficult to categorize. He did not fit
comfortably within a specific disciplinary framework, nor did his work follow a
cohesive trajectory. He described his intellectual enterprise as a 'critical history of
thought'.[42] His work consistently revolves around a particular set of concerns to
do with systems of thought and the ways in which knowledge is produced and
maintained through discourse. The political rebellions of the 1960s turned his
attention towards the exercise of power, and his subsequent body of work has been
described as the study of 'how systems of ideas become systems of power'.[43]
Foucault's writings also have a strong historical dimension: he wrote substantive
histories of madness, the prison, and sexuality, although historians have criticized
his 'cavalier use of historical records', and 'lax' documentation.[44] Perhaps, as one
commentator has suggested, 'all of Foucault's major works are histories of a sort,
which is enough to make him a historian of a sort'.[45] And indeed many historians

have found aspects of Foucault's approach to history, in particular his concept of 'discursive formations', to be very productive.

## ▶ Discourse

The term 'discourse' has a long history, and traditionally simply designated a formal discussion of a topic, a treatise or a homily. There are many contemporary definitions of discourse reflecting the range of approaches taken by discourse analysts. The French linguist Émile Benveniste (1902–76) defined discourse very broadly as 'any utterance involving a speaker and a hearer, and an intention, on the part of the speaker, of influencing the hearer'. In practice discourse may:

> refer to an extended piece of text, or its verbal equivalent, that forms a unit of analysis. . . . The term is widely, and often very loosely, used to describe any organized body or corpus of statements and utterances governed by rules and conventions of which the user is largely unconscious.[46]

However, the term 'discourse' is utilized across the theoretical spectrum, in both empiricist and poststructural accounts of the past, with very different conceptual implications. In the former, discourses may be defined as a product of the active agency of human beings in response to the material world. Empiricists tend to define discourses as 'frames or cognitive schemata . . . the conscious strategic efforts by groups of people to fashion shared understandings of the world and of themselves that legitimate and motivate collective action'. [47] In this definition it is the social and material world that shapes discourse.

But poststructuralists proceed on a contrary understanding: that language and symbolic structures shape subjective understanding of the social and material world. This is the essence of Foucault's definition of discourse: discourses are 'practices that systematically form the objects of which they speak'.[48] From this perspective the thinking human being disappears, and is replaced by a subject, or rather subject position, created by discourse. In the work of poststructuralists, it is argued, the 'self' has been 'reduced to an entirely constructed, and therefore empty and wholly plastic, nodal point in a discursive or cultural system'.[49] The death of individualism or, as Foucault put it, 'death of man', consequently undermined a whole raft of concepts central to conventional historical accounts of the past: for example, agency, intentionality, and experience. As has been pointed out, 'without a purposive historical actor and any concept of intentionality, it is impossible to establish a ground from which the individual can fashion his or her destiny on the basis of his or her experience of the world'.[50] While many historians could not accept this, Stedman Jones suggested that Foucault's position represented continuity with earlier conceptions of the human mind, such as that of *mentalité*:

> this relegation of the author or historical agent to the mere occupation of 'a subject position' in the new conception of discourse was not much more than the accentuation of a long tradition of emphasis upon historically situated unconscious and habitual mental processes, associated particularly with the work of Lucien Febvre and encapsulated in the *Annales* conception of 'mentalité'.[51]

Foucault was particularly interested in the idea of discursive formations, that is 'groups of statements in which it is possible to find a pattern of regularity defined in terms of order, correlation, position and function'.[52] *The Archaeology of Knowledge* (1969), for example, focuses upon the epistemological foundations of particular discourses. Foucault uses the term 'archaeology' to 'mean an investigation into that which makes certain forms of thought possible and even inescapable': the organization of bodies of knowledge around a central 'stratum of rules of which its thinkers are not consciously aware'.[53] Foucault called this the *episteme*, 'the system of concepts that defines knowledge for a given intellectual era'.[54] In other words, he argued that the same conceptual structure underlay different contemporaneous bodies of knowledge. In the Renaissance, for example, 'the world was governed by the *episteme* of "similitude": the world was a book and obeyed a vast syntactic system based upon a system of similarities and correspondences'. In contrast, during the classical age (circa 1650–1800), knowledge was organized around 'a general mathematical science of order . . . a more empirical system of classification'.[55] Modernity, he suggests, is the 'Age of Man' – when 'man' becomes the 'object of his own knowledge'.[56] These *epistemes* were 'mental grids' through which information and experience were processed, and ensured that individuals could only perceive through 'the already encoded eye'.[57]

There are two points that should be made here. First of all, Foucault argued that the concept of *episteme* is very different from, for example, *Weltanschauung* (worldview) or *Zeitgeist* (spirit of an age). 'I do not seek to detect, starting from diverse signs, the unitary spirit of an epoch. . . . I have collated different discourses and described their clusters and relations.'[58] The term *episteme* derives from the Greek word for knowledge, and therefore denotes the underlying **epistemology** (the basis of knowledge) rather than collective representations or beliefs. Secondly, Foucault acknowledged that abrupt ruptures occur in the underlying *episteme*, although he did not elaborate a theory of epistemic breaks and cultural change. It has been suggested that Foucault was reacting against the teleological framework found among traditional historians whereby the present becomes the logical and desirable outcome of the past.[59]

## ▶ Knowledge/Power

However, the archaeological method of explicating the structures of discourse did not enable Foucault to pursue questions that began to interest him – the ways in which discourses (knowledge) operated socially as systems of power. He abandoned the attempt to 'work out a theory of rule-governed systems of discursive practices', and redirected the archaeology of discourse towards new ends:[60]

> It is true that I became quite involved with the question of power. It soon appeared to me that, while the human subject is placed in relations of production and signification, he is equally placed in power relations which are very complex. Now, it seemed to me that economic history and theory provided a good instrument for relations of production; that linguistics and semiotics offered instruments for studying relations of signification; but for power relations we had no tools of study.[61]

Discourse was Foucault's key to understanding power relations, since 'it is in discourse that power and knowledge are joined together'.[62] His conception of power was broad and diffuse: 'Power is everywhere; not because it embraces everything, but because it comes from everywhere . . . there is no binary and all-encompassing opposition between rulers and ruled at the root of power relations.'[63] In order to explicate the relationship between knowledge and power, Foucault borrowed a particular insight from Nietzsche, 'that the search for knowledge is also an expression of a will to power over other people'; and a technique called 'genealogy'.[64] The subject of contested definitions, 'genealogy' may be described as a development upon the earlier concept of 'archaeology'; it is a 'form of historical analysis which describes events in the past but without explicitly making causal connections'.[65] In this sense Foucault's approach is very different from the conventional history of madness, for example, which traced the development of knowledge about the mind as a developmental and progressive process.

Let us take *Madness and Civilization* (1961) to demonstrate Foucault's approach to the production of knowledge. The book begins with a description of the leper houses (lazar houses) in Europe during the Middle Ages. Placed on the edges of communities and cities, tens of thousands of leprosariums kept the sick at bay. Then, suddenly, in the fourteenth century the lazar houses began to empty, the consequence of the segregation and isolation, and the break with traditional sources of infection in the East. Three centuries later, he argues, 'often, in these same places, the formulas of exclusion would be repeated. . . . Poor vagabonds, criminals, and "deranged minds" would take the part played by the leper.'[66] In the few opening pages, therefore, Foucault foreshadows the 'twin themes of spatial exclusion and cultural integration' that are the focus of the book.[67] The framework shaping this study is not one of scientific progress. Madness, Foucault suggests, is not a fixed condition but is constructed differently during particular periods of history. During the 'Age of Reason', madness became the counterpoint to reason, with clear distinctions made between the two. Human behaviour that would once have been regarded by the Church in terms of visions or spiritual possession – hallucinating, hearing imagined voices, or speaking in tongues – was conceptualized anew:

> In the Renaissance, madness was present everywhere and mingled with every experience by its images or its dangers. During the classical period, madness was shown, but on the other side of bars; if present, it was at a distance, under the eyes of a reason that no longer felt any relation to it and that would not compromise itself by too close a resemblance.[68]

Secondly, Foucault emphasizes the 'material and institutional practices' that support powerful discourses.[69] The incarceration of the poor, infirm, and mad from the seventeenth century onwards is linked to the earlier isolation of the lepers. In other words, the availability of such 'houses of confinement' contributed to the institutionalization of the 'socially useless' from the seventeenth century onwards.[70] In *The Birth of the Clinic: An Archaeology of Medical Perception* (1963), and *Discipline and Punish: The Birth of the Prison* (1975) Foucault continued his exploration of the ways in which human beings are constituted, for example, as mad or sane, delinquent or law-abiding, through discourses within psychiatry and criminal science.[71]

Over the past twenty years the Foucauldian approach to discourse has dominated some fields of enquiry, particularly feminist cultural history and postcolonial history. The appeal of the 'linguistic turn' to a new generation of scholars has been attributed to its capacity to 'de-essentialize' concepts such as male and female, or black and white. If these concepts are discursively constructed they are open to challenge and alternative readings.[72] The de-essentialization of conceptual language also derived considerable intellectual impetus from the analytic method called '**deconstruction**', pioneered by another French poststructuralist philosopher, Jacques Derrida (1930–2004). Born in Algeria, Derrida also attended the École Normale Supérieure and studied under Foucault. Because Derrida's writing is very difficult to understand, and since destabilizing meaning is one purpose of 'deconstruction', it may be better to attempt an explanation rather than a definition.

## ▶ Deconstruction

The term 'deconstruction', invented by Derrida in the 1960s, describes a method of unpacking the implicit and unconscious meanings of signs. At the heart of

Derrida's approach is the assertion of semiotic instability: signs generate 'endless, undecidable chains of meanings'.[73] For our discussion here, the most important dimension of 'deconstruction' is its critique of binary oppositions within language. As we saw earlier, dichotomous thought is central to linguistic structuralism: binary oppositions were at the core of both Saussure's theory of signs and the cultural systems of Lévi-Strauss. Meaning, in Saussure's linguistic model, 'depended upon difference: meaning was relational, fixed only through opposition. We know what black is because we know what white is.'[74]

In *Of Grammatology* (1976) Derrida argues that these dualities of thought are not neutral, that one term is privileged as the original and authentic and the second is more derivative. The goal of deconstruction is to unpack those hierarchical conceptual oppositions. There are three steps in the deconstructive process: first, the hierarchy of meaning implicit within dichotomous thinking is revealed; secondly, the hierarchy is inverted, or reversed. Finally, one of the terms should be displaced and replaced with a new definition. There is, with the Derridean method, no finality to this process, only infinite, unresolvable, sequences of meaning. Despite the difficulties of Derrida's writing, and the strength of the critical response, Eley argues that 'deconstruction's basic program – at its simplest, "a reading which involves seizing upon [the text's] inconsistencies and contradictions to break up the idea of a unified whole" – has become very commonplace'.[75]

'I do not believe that anyone can detect by *reading*, if I do not myself declare it, that I am a "French Algerian",' wrote Jacques Derrida in 1998.[76] Despite this disclaimer, it has been suggested that poststructuralism's historical moment was less May 1968 than the Algerian War of Independence. Foucault lived and taught in Tunisia during his early adulthood, and Derrida was born in Algeria. In the case of the latter, it has been argued that this experience shaped his subsequent intellectual preoccupations:

> neither French or Algerian, [Derrida was] always anti-nationalist and cosmopolitan, critical of western ethnocentrism from *Of Grammatology's* very first page, preoccupied with justice and injustice, developed deconstruction as a procedure for intellectual and cultural decolonization. . . . The surgical operation of deconstruction was always directed at the identity of the ontological violence that sustains the western metaphysical and ideological systems . . . a structural relation of power that had to be teased apart if it was ever to be overturned.[77]

Whether the key moment in the development of poststructural theory is May 1968 or the Algerian War of Independence, the concept of discourse and the method of textual reading through deconstruction have together generated an extensive literature within cultural history exploring closely linked discursive constructions such as the colonial subject, and gender. Let us begin with the first, and a seminal book that generated a new field – that of postcolonial studies.

## ▶ Orientalism

*Orientalism,* published in 1978, by Edward Said, a Palestinian academic based in the United States, analyses French and British colonial discourse on the Orient and, for the first time, linked 'culture inexorably with colonialism'.[78] Said explicitly acknowledged his debt to Foucault, explaining that:

> I have found it useful here to employ Michel Foucault's notion of a discourse . . . to identify Orientalism. My contention is that without examining Orientalism as a discourse one cannot possibly understand the enormously systematic discipline by which European culture was able to manage – and even produce – the Orient politically, sociologically, militarily, ideologically, scientifically, and imaginatively during the post-Enlightenment period.[79]

The management and production of the Orient – defined as 'adjacent to Europe . . . the place of Europe's greatest and richest and oldest colonies' – was achieved through a discourse of 'Orientalism'. The writings of scholars, novelists and politicians, Said argued, created a 'body of theory and practice in which, for many generations, there has been considerable material investment. Continued investment made Orientalism . . . an accepted grid for filtering through the Orient into Western consciousness.'[80] It should be noted that critics have drawn attention to Said's selective use of sources, which neglect the diversity of perspectives that in practice existed within the discourse on 'Orientalism'.[81]

Said made two fundamental arguments about the nature of Orientalism.[82] First of all, he suggests that Western scholars constructed a binary opposition between East and West, one in which inferior and antagonistic characteristics were enshrined in the concept of the Orient. Essentialist representations of non-Europeans, for whom Said uses the term 'the other', included a set of indispensable characteristics: politically, as unchanging/despotic, or socially, as sensual/cruel. This is the core theoretical point, and has implications for any scholar seeking to represent another culture. Is it possible to 'escape procedures of dichotomizing, restructuring and textualizing in the making of interpretative statements about foreign cultures and traditions?'[83] Secondly, Said addressed the relationship between this 'regime of truth' (to use Foucault's term) and imperialism. He argues that the fundamental tenets of Orientalism became a 'science of imperialism', used to justify the exploitation and domination by European powers.

After the publication of *Orientalism,* colonialism could no longer be regarded only in terms of economic or military conquest. But Said's implied hegemony of orientalist discourse has undergone revision in the light of new studies revealing contradictions between discursive prescription and practice in colonial contexts, and instability and ambivalence within colonial discourse.[84] The postcolonial theorist Homi Bhabha, for example, found discursive constructions of difference in nineteenth-century British writing on India to be uncertain and ambivalent.[85] Colonized subjects were 'almost the same, but not quite'; simultaneously both 'culturally assimilable' and 'amenable to colonization'.[86] Bhabha has characterized cultural relations between the colonizer and colonized in terms of 'hybridity' rather than difference, arguing that cultural encounter and conflict disturbed settled identities constructed around binary oppositions, creating space on the margins for new discourses. Other studies of cultural encounter, such as Richard White's concept of a 'middle ground' in Native American and English relations in the late seventeenth century, have also sought to move beyond the binary oppositions of colonialism.[87]

The difficulties of understanding the impact of cultural encounter upon human subjectivity and expression are reflected in *Trickster Travels: A Sixteenth-Century Muslim Between Worlds*, in which Natalie Zemon Davis examines the life and writings of al-Hasan al-Wassan, a sixteenth-century traveller and diplomat from Fez captured by a Spanish pirate and presented to the Pope in 1518. While in Italy, al-Hasan al-Wassan converted to Christianity (possibly under duress and to escape prison) and wrote several manuscripts, one of which, *La Descrittione dell'Africa*, became a bestseller. The surviving text is the basis for Davis's carefully contextualized analysis of al-Hasan al-Wassan's 'strategies and mentality' as he balanced the exigencies of his situation with perceptive observation and reflection upon two cultures. Hoping to return home, al-Wassan had to write with two audiences in mind, carefully balancing what he could and could not say. Moving back and forth between descriptions and commentary on Europe and then Africa, is it possible to interpret 'his double vision'? Davis suggests the key lies early in the book, where al-Wassan invents a bird story about ruse and invention. The narrative of a bird that 'escapes obligation and blame by claiming different identities' had resonance in both Italian and Arabic popular stories, and in it he built 'a bridge for himself, one that he could cross in either direction'. His text, Davis suggests, reflects multiple strategies, 'dissimulation, performance, translation, and the quest for peaceful enlightenment'.[88]

## ▶ Gender

A second area of cultural history in which poststructuralist approaches have been deeply influential, with close discursive links to the postcolonial subject, has been that of **gender** history. The influence of feminist history in preparing the ground for the 'linguistic turn' was acknowledged earlier in this chapter. Struggling against the biological essentialism that permeated the wider historical profession, feminist historians were to be particularly receptive to poststructuralist perspectives. As the literary theorist Terry Eagleton has pointed out:

> For all the binary oppositions which post-structuralism sought to undo, the hierarchical opposition between men and women was perhaps the most virulent. Certainly it seemed the most perdurable: there was no time in history at which a good half of the human race had not been banished and subjected as a defective being, an alien inferior.[89]

Reconceptualizing contemporary historical paradigms that excluded women could only be achieved, Joan Scott argued in an influential article published in 1986, through transformation of the concept of gender. Although the term 'gender' had historicized relationships between the sexes, it nonetheless perpetuated the idea that gender was the study 'of things related to women'. The concept itself needed to encompass the much deeper gendered discourses that shaped social and cultural relationships, and in particular relationships of power. Until it did so, gender theory would have little to offer the study of political or economic history. Gender, as an analytic category, needed to pay 'attention to signifying systems, that is, to the ways societies represent gender, use it to articulate the rules of social relationships or construct the meaning of experience'. In order to establish the first, she suggested, historians should investigate symbolic representations, normative concepts, social institutions and organizations, and the ways gendered identities are constructed.[90]

Gender theory encompasses the construction of both masculinity and femininity, and has been employed particularly fruitfully to illuminate relationships of power between colonizer and colonized.[91] An example of this approach may be found in Mrinalini Sinha's *Colonial Masculinity: The 'Many Englishman' and the 'Effeminate Bengali' in the Late Nineteenth Century* (1995). Sinha combines a focus upon the language of colonial masculinity with attention to other categories such as class/caste, race or nation. The intersection of all these is particularly evident in the Ilbert Bill controversy. In 1883 a bill was introduced into the Legislative Council that gave 'native officials in the colonial administrative service limited criminal jurisdiction of European British subjects . . .'. A mutiny by Anglo-Indians followed, in which a gendered colonial discourse around the concept of 'effeminacy' was used to justify racial hierarchy. According to a senior Anglo-Indian official, for example, the Bengalis were disqualified for political enfranchisement because they possessed 'essentially feminine characteristic'. Whereas such characteristics were 'worthy of honour' among women, they turned Bengali men into 'objects of ridicule'. Sinha concludes that opposition to the Ilbert Bill 'substituted for a straight-forward defence of racial exclusivity a supposedly more "natural" gender hierarchy between "manly" and "unmanly" men'.[92] Sinha's study is an excellent example of the 'new ways of theorizing difference': difference 'not as what people intrinsically *are*, but what they are ascribed . . . in the context of domination'.[93]

It has been argued that one consequence of the 'displacement of sex by gender' is that the 'discursive body has figured more prominently in the last decade of gender history.'[94] Let us look at one key example from this body of work, *Making Sex: Body and Gender from the Greeks to Freud* (1990), by Thomas Laqueur. In the late eighteenth century, Laqueur argues, the construction of sexual, biological, difference underwent a fundamental change. Up until this point, and from ancient times, the body – both male and female – was a one-sex model. Male and female reproductive organs were perceived as one, with those of women defined as 'inverted, and hence less perfect' than those of men.[95] The one-sex model persisted over centuries of social, political and cultural change, and one reason for its durability, Laqueur suggests, is that it linked sex to power, and demonstrated what was 'already massively evident in culture more generally: *man* is the measure of all things, and woman does not exist as an ontologically distinct category . . . the standard of the human body and its representations is the male body'.[96]

However, in the late eighteenth century, Laqueur reports, 'sex as we know it was invented'. The one-sex model was replaced by a model of 'complementary difference, which stressed the binary oppositions between the two physiologies'.[97] In addition, the new bodily discourse increasingly tied woman's nature to her reproductive biology. 'Women's bodies', Laqueur writes, '. . . came to bear an enormous new weight of meaning. Two sexes, in other words, were invented as a new foundation for gender.' The reasons behind the change, he suggests, were twofold: the new epistemological status of nature and science, in combination with the ending a century earlier of the *episteme* of similitudes; and a political context that had become a battleground between men and women, and between feminists and antifeminists.[98] The point that Laqueur seeks to make is that sexual difference is a discursive formation:

> Two sexes are not the necessary, natural consequence of corporeal difference. Nor, for that matter, is one sex. The ways in which sexual difference have been imagined in the past are largely unconstrained by what was actually known about this or that bit of anatomy . . . and derive instead from the rhetorical exigencies of the moment . . . basically the content of talk about sexual difference is unfettered by fact, and is as free as mind's play.[99]

## ► Conclusion

In conclusion, let us briefly consider some of the critiques of the poststructuralist approach. These tend to fall around three poles. The first rejects the 'crude functionalist notion of social control' that can be attributed to Foucault's theory. Efforts to emancipate or improve are not necessarily also attempts to control or punish.[100] Foucault's position, it has been argued, ignores aspects of human history driven by 'civic humanism' and comparable movements.[101] A second critique revolves around the absence within Foucauldian analysis of a theory of epistemic or cultural change. Foucault identified abrupt ruptures, or epistemic breaks, but rejected any concept of linear development in human thought. Each period, or *episteme*, was severed from its predecessor. He never succeeded in explaining, for example, how the transformation in the language of 'reason, self-consciousness and social explanation' in the late eighteenth century could occur.[102] This, as we have seen, is a repeated refrain concerning cultural history as a whole.

The final critique resonates with the position taken by Bakhtin, discussed earlier in the chapter, that language should be understood within the social context, and as the product of verbal interaction. The focus upon a specifically abstract Saussurean version of language (*langue*), rather than the expression through speech (*parole*), neglects the gap between the semiotic code on the one hand, and the particular expression of it on the other.[103] It has been suggested that more attention should be paid to actual discursive practice, thereby bringing the active agency of human beings back into discourse analysis.[104] In the next chapter we turn to the oral expression of language, but in the context of another dimension of the mind, that of memory. Theories concerning individual remembering also wrestle with the role of the unconscious, narrative, and the relationship between public discourse and private consciousness.

# 5 Remembering

It is only comparatively recently that cultural historians have begun to investigate the ways in which, as individuals and collectivities, we remember the past. In recent years, however, the concept of memory has become 'a leading term, recently perhaps *the* leading term, in cultural history.'[1] A rich body of cultural history has explored many dimensions of memory, from the life narratives of individuals to the collective memorialisation of war and the preservation of 'heritage'. In the process the definition and usefulness of 'individual memory' and 'collective memory' as concepts have come under critical scrutiny. While this has generated a lively contemporary debate among historians, there is little agreement about the meaning of these terms.[2]

## ▶ Memory

What is memory? The Dutch psychologist Douwe Draaisma has described the 'churnings of the metaphor mill [that have] projected constantly changing images of our representations of memory. Memory was once a wax tablet, codex or magic slate, then again an abbey or theatre, sometimes a forest, or on other occasions a treasure chest, aviary or warehouse.' Since the middle of the nineteenth century, the **metaphors** have been drawn primarily from the new technologies: first of all photography and film, then, after the Second World War, the computer.[3] Just as the word 'history' has two quite separate meanings – that which actually happened in the past, and the historians' construction of the same events – so too does the concept of memory. Memory may be used to describe both the biological processes and the written or verbal expression of the remembered past. Understanding the storage and retrieval processes of memory in the brain is the province of a developing synthesis between molecular biology and cognitive neuroscience.[4] Psychologists and others distinguish between many different types of memory: short- and long-term; auditory or iconic; semantic, motor or visual memory. In contrast, historians investigate the expression and representation of the remembered past by living individuals and collectivities of people. This is why this chapter is a study of remembering (and forgetting) rather than of memory itself.

Nonetheless, there is common ground between the neuroscientists and historians engaged in the study of memory. Both share a conviction, first of all, that memory is absolutely central to our sense of self as human beings. As neuroscientist Steven Rose has emphasized, 'memory defines who we are and shapes the way we act more closely than any other single aspect of our personhood . . . lose your memory and you, as *you*, cease to exist . . . '.[5] Secondly, they would agree that memory cannot be 'passive or literal recordings of reality . . . we do not store judgement-free snapshots of our past experiences but rather hold on to the meaning, sense, and emotions these experiences provided us'.[6] Daniel Schacter argues persuasively that while memories are 'subjectively compelling and influential', they are equally 'fragile', and subject to various kinds of distortion.[7] Remembering, all would agree, is an 'active, selective, and constructive process'.[8]

But there are limits to what we know about this 'active, selective, and constructive' process of remembering. In 2005, Rose sadly acknowledged 'the inability of my own profession, despite the millions invested and the sophistication of our techniques, to understand better the peculiarities of memory'. Psychologists only began referring to the part of memory in which we store our personal experiences as 'autobiographical memory' in the 1980s. Rose regrets that we do not know the answers to many simple questions about everyday memory: why our memories of ourselves as children are so profoundly different in quality from those we have as adults; why at seventy years of age we remember more clearly what happened to us in our twenties than in our fifties; or what happens when our memories decay.[9] What we do know, as Draaisma points out, is that:

> autobiographical memory recalls and forgets at the same time. It is as if you are having the notes of your life taken by an obstreperous company secretary, who meticulously documents those things you would rather forget and during your finest hours pretends to be industriously at work when actually he still has the cap of his pen screwed on.[10]

The shared agreement concerning the value-laden, partial and unpredictable nature of memory led orthodox empirical historians to draw a clear distinction between history and memory, 'the first self-conscious and analytic, the second involuntary and subjective'.[11] Some historians seriously questioned the value of memory for historical research altogether.[12] But others argue that the distinction itself is false. In 1989 Peter Burke, for example, questioned the validity of this epistemological divide, arguing that 'neither memories nor histories seem objective any longer. In both cases we are learning to take account of conscious or unconscious selection, interpretation and distortion. In both cases, this selection, interpretation and distortion is socially conditioned.'[13] Burke's riposte to empiricists emphasized the socially constructed nature of representations of the past, whether generated by memory or by conventional historical methodology.

Before turning to the early twentieth-century theoretical scaffolding that continues to shape our current understanding of the processes of remembering, we should return briefly to a point made earlier in this introduction. Only individuals can remember in the physiological sense, and they can only directly recall events experienced or occurring during their lifetime. Nonetheless, cultural historians are also interested in how collectivities of people, including whole societies, 'remember' the past. In this case, the definition of remembering is expanded both spatially and temporally outside the boundaries of individual human experience. In practice, historians of individual and collective memory fall into two discrete camps, and there is relatively little intellectual engagement between them. Most would agree, however, that there is no linear or aggregative relationship between individual memory and collective memory (indeed, the two may often co-exist in a state of tension).[14] Secondly, historians interested in collective memory focus more upon objectified cultural memory: for example, the production, display or representation of cultural artefacts, heritage or rituals. This body of work on collective memory will be the subject of the following chapter. But first we must examine remembering as the communication of individual experience, narrated within particular social and cultural contexts.

## ▶ Early theorists of remembering

Our contemporary understandings of the nature of remembering and forgetting were, in fact, *re*discovered towards the end of the twentieth century. Many of the ideas currently underpinning contemporary memory studies were first developed in the very early years of the twentieth century. Pioneering work on memory by Richard Semon, published in 1904, developed the idea of the 'engram', the memory trace, and emphasized the importance of the conditions under which memories were retrieved.[15] But the most influential ideas, which later resurfaced in different guises, were developed by the psychologist Frederic Bartlett and the sociologist Maurice Halbwachs, researching and writing in the 1920s and 1930s. Both men were either taught or influenced early in their careers by academic mentors whose interests lay in the relationship between human behaviour and beliefs and social and cultural environments: in Bartlett's case, the psychologist and anthropologist W. R. D. Rivers, and in Halbwach's, the sociologist Émile Durkheim.[16] While both Bartlett and Halbwachs were to move beyond, and in some cases away from, these early mentors, their research into memory retained a contextual, cultural focus.

Frederic Bartlett (1886–1969) was the first Professor of Experimental Psychology at Cambridge in 1931, and between 1914 and 1939 his investigations into perception and memory broke new ground in a variety of ways.[17] In terms of methodology he rejected the type of experimental memory tests common among his contemporaries, in favour of 'ecologically valid' tasks that he believed were better reflections of real life.[18] Instead of using the repetition of nonsense syllables favoured by some of his peers, Bartlett asked his subjects to examine pictures, or repeat folk tales that they had read some time before. The extent to which this approach was more appropriate is debatable: 'one might argue that having participants read a difficult Kathlamet folk story twice then asking them to recall it 15 minutes or 10 years later does not exactly fit his own arguments for ecological validity'.[19] But the approach forced Bartlett into developing a new explanatory theory for his memory data. Bartlett found that individuals sought to make sense of the Kathlamet story in terms of their own cultural understandings, for example, changing words or excluding dimensions of the story they found incomprehensible. He concluded that human memory 'is an active, selective and constructive process . . . not a passive reaction or a mechanical reproduction of the external information and stimuli'.[20] In 1932 Bartlett outlined his conclusions in his best known book on the subject, *Remembering*.

Bartlett's experiments suggested that completely accurate recall was comparatively rare, and he came to the conclusion that remembering is a constructive, or reconstructive, process in which three specific mental faculties come into play. These three dimensions of memory are schema, images, and attitude, and he sums these up as follows:

> Remembering is not the re-excitation of innumerable fixed, lifeless and fragmentary traces. It is an imaginative reconstruction, or construction, built out of the relation of our attitude towards a whole active mass of organised past reactions or experience [schema], and to a little outstanding detail which commonly appears in image or in language form.[21]

Let us briefly look at each of these concepts in turn. Schemata are 'the mental representations of generic knowledge in the long-term memory'.[22] Schemata are abstract, and exist at the level of the unconscious; for example, the generic idea of a 'room' with windows and doors, floor and ceiling. In contrast, images are the traces of a specific memory, for example, a particular room from one's childhood. 'Images . . . allowed the generic schemata to be individualised and provided the outstanding details around which the reconstructive process would build recall of a particular incident.'[23]

Finally, the third concept of attitude encompasses all the ways in which individuals relate themselves to the remembered event. Attitude consists of the feelings about remembered individual experiences; it includes emotions, but is not confined to these. 'Attitude', Bartlett wrote, is 'very largely a matter of feeling, or affect. We say that it is characterised by doubt, hesitation, surprise, astonishment, confidence, dislike, repulsion and so on.' These feelings, Bartlett argued, were usually the first dimension to emerge, and he believed that the subsequent recollection was 'a construction, made largely on the basis of this attitude, and its general effect is that of a justification of the attitude'.[24] Attitude is the concept that explains the 'purposive and intentional aspects of remembering', and allowed Bartlett to explain individual differences in recall in terms of 'the person's basic personality traits, character and temperament'.[25]

In the last part of *Remembering* Bartlett emphasizes the social and cultural contextual factors of memory and remembering. He focuses upon two ways in which the social milieu profoundly shapes the individual's public recollections. The first concerns the collective cultural meanings that shape schema, image and attitude in memory:

> both the manner and matter of recall are often predominantly determined by social influences. In perceiving, in imaging, in remembering proper, and in constructive work, the passing fashion of the group, the social catch-word, the prevailing approved general interest, the persistent social custom and institution set the stage and direct the action.[26]

Bartlett argues that the audience plays a critical role in controlling what can, and cannot, be said, and that particular types of narration will invariably dominate recall: 'the comic, the pathetic, and the dramatic, for example, will tend to spring into prominence. There is social control from the auditors to the narrator'.[27] In this sense, individual memory for Bartlett almost appears to coalesce with collective memory, given the power he attributes to the social context. Nonetheless, he agreed with his contemporary Maurice Halbwachs that this was 'memory *in* the group, not memory *of* the group', and that no evidence of group memory as such had been found. 'Social direction and control of recall – memory within the group – are obvious,' he wrote, 'but a literal memory *of* the group cannot, at present at least, be demonstrated.'[28] Bartlett's conclusions concerning the nature of memory closely parallel, in a number of important respects, those of Maurice Halbwachs, to whose work we now turn.

Maurice Halbwachs (1877–1945) began systematically exploring the social construction of memory as an oral discourse in the 1920s. Many of the preoccupations of the later generation of cultural historians may be discerned in his final study of memory, *The Collective Memory,* published posthumously in 1950. Halbwachs's approach to the subject of memory was influenced by the sociologist Émile Durkheim, and the two shared a close working relationship. Durkheim was interested in the processes through which social cohesion is achieved, and in the *function* performed by cultural and social practices, integrating the individual into the group and creating social harmony. Halbwachs believed that memory performed a similar socially integrative function.

Halbwachs argued, first of all, that memory was irreducibly socially determined; at all times, from childhood through to adulthood, memories were created within specific social contexts and through active engagement with other human beings.[29] He rejected the concept of any purely individual conscious state, likening such a belief to assuming that 'a heavy object, suspended in air by means of a number of very thin and interlaced wires, actually rests in the void where it holds itself up'.[30] The thin and interlaced wires of his metaphor are the relationships, beliefs and experiences shared with others in various social groups. Secondly, he argued that within any one group – a family, a class at the lycée, or a group of friends – the most durable collective memories tended to be those held by the greatest number. Reflecting Durkheim's influence, Halbwachs also suggested that the need for an 'affective community' ensured that individuals remembered primarily those memories that harmonized with those of others.

Halbwachs accepted that there were differences between what he preferred to call 'autobiographical memory' and 'historical memory'. These two types of memory, for example, did not share the same temporal or spatial dimensions. The relationship between historical and personal time was tenuous. Only in retrospect was it possible for individuals to link their own memories to the 'historic' events that had occurred during their lifetime. Making this link often entailed a leap of the imagination:

> During my life, my national society has been theater for a number of events I say 'I remember', events that I know about only from newspapers or the testimony of those directly involved. ... These events have deeply influenced national thought, not only because their tradition endures, very much alive in region, province, political party, occupation, class, even certain families or persons who experienced them firsthand. For me they are conceptions, symbols. I picture them pretty much as others do. I can imagine them, but I cannot remember them.[31]

Halbwachs, therefore, made three particularly important arguments about the relationship between individual memory and the social context in which it takes shape, and all three share a great deal of common ground with the ideas of Frederic Bartlett. The first is the interdependent relationship between individual and collective memory. This is reflected in his often-repeated dictum that, 'while the collective memory endures and draws strength from its base in a coherent body of people, it is individuals as group members who remember'.[32] In other words, turning the phrase around, while individuals remember, it is the social group that determines what memories will be commemorated. Secondly, Halbwachs is insistent that individual memories are the product of social engagement and experience; that the desire to belong to a social group reinforces those individual memories that accord with those of others. Finally, Halbwachs drew attention to ways in which individuals incorporate into their memories, through imagination, events that they have not directly experienced themselves.

## ▶ Critiques

Both Bartlett and Halbwachs drew heavily upon the functionalist ideas dominant during their lifetime, with the consequence that their interpretations of individual memory are highly determinist. Bartlett emphasized the functional properties of each dimension of memory: schema, image and attitude.[33] While the concept of attitude was used to explain differences in recall, Bartlett linked it to personality traits and temperament. His theory appears to leave little role for conscious intellectual engagement with the past. Halbwachs focused upon the power of the social group to influence how the past is remembered and his theory appears dependent upon highly cohesive social groups. Bartlett and Halbwachs primarily saw remembering as a socially integrative process, neglecting the role of conflicting memories as agents of change.

One of the criticisms of Halbwachs's findings is that individual memory becomes overdetermined. Is there any space for individual consciousness? What happens to memories that do not fit in with the dominant social memory? This has been identified as a major problem for those wishing to build upon Halbwachs's conceptualization of remembering: is it possible 'to elaborate a conception of memory which, while doing full justice to the collective side of one's conscious life, does not render the individual a sort of automaton, passively obeying the interiorised collective will'?[34] Some have rejected the significance of individual memory altogether. For example, the sociologist Michael Schudson argues that since memory can only be expressed through the 'cultural construction of language in 'socially structured patterns of recall', in the most important sense all memory is collective cultural memory.[35] Certainly separation of individual memory from the collective social and cultural context cannot be sustained, for individual memory is composed within specific environments that shape its very essence. But these social and cultural contexts are riven with competing values, hierarchies, and conflicts. Furthermore, no one individual shares exactly the same life experiences as any other. The value of personal memories, as we shall see, lies in the attempt to make sense of, and reconcile, unique material and subjective experiences.

There was little immediate critical engagement with Bartlett and Halbwach's pioneering work on memory, and interest generally in their work lapsed for nearly fifty years. Nonetheless, many of their insights concerning the constructed nature of our remembered past and the importance of the social and cultural contexts within which we remember now resonate throughout the work of contemporary cultural historians. The role of culture in shaping recall, through the influence of myths and legends, narrative forms, and public discourse, is well documented. But the sociocultural determinism of Halbwachs and Bartlett is less evident in contemporary studies, where dissenting voices and alternative narratives break through dominant historical narratives. Both Bartlett and Halbwachs focused upon the oral transmission of memory between individuals and within small social groups, and so it is to the work of oral historians we will now turn. However, establishing both the validity and the importance of life narratives as historical evidence was (and remains) an uphill battle within the profession.

As a consequence of the democratization of higher education in the Western world in the 1960s, women, ethnic-minority, and working-class historians began to write the histories of previously marginalized groups. This new generation of postwar historians substantially shifted the focus of conventional historical enquiry. Lack of documentary records in these areas of enquiry turned some of the younger members of the historical profession towards living repositories of historical experience, a process facilitated by the new recording technologies. This early oral history often sought to extend the methodology of historical empiricism to the field of memory, seeking factual and representative information relating to working and family lives.[36] Other historians published edited transcripts of rich oral testimonies.[37] A great deal of valuable social history was generated in the fields of labour, family, and women's history.[38] Nonetheless, oral history had trenchant critics among professional historians. While able to accept the revisionist nature of orthodox empirical history, the critics often regarded the same revisionist tendencies in memory as an insuperable flaw. The intrinsically subjective and individual nature of remembered human experience was perceived as antithetical to the conventional historical goals of factual verification and the elucidation of common patterns in the past. Oral historians struggled to address these criticisms, on the critics' own terrain.

## ▶ Subjectivity

The way out of this impasse, through recognition of the specific, and unique, features of memory, came in a ground-breaking study by Luisa Passerini, published in 1979.[39] Seeking to understand memories of working-class life under the fascists in Turin during the 1920s and 1930s, Luisa Passerini argued that historians, preoccupied only with the factual content of oral testimonies, were fundamentally missing the 'peculiar specificity of oral material'.[40] 'The raw material of oral history', she wrote, ' . . . is pre-eminently an expression and representation of culture, and therefore includes not only literal narrations but also the dimensions of memory, ideology and subconscious desires.' These she grouped together under one conceptual label, that of subjectivity:

> By this I wish to connote that area of symbolic activity which includes cognitive, cultural and psychological aspects. The terms used to define this area more narrowly are generally confused and vague because of the overlapping meanings and subtle differences of emphasis which have been attached to their typical conceptualisations, such as mentality, ideology, culture, world-view (*Weltanschauung*), and consciousness. In comparison with these, subjectivity has the advantage of being a term sufficiently elastic to include both the aspects of spontaneous subject being . . . contained and represented by attitude, behaviour and language, as well as other forms of awareness . . . such as the sense of identity, consciousness of oneself and more considered forms of intellectual activity.[41]

Passerini proceeded to illustrate the ability of 'subjectivity' to generate insights about the past, discussing two particular dimensions of her oral material. These were the silences, and the jokes and anecdotes. First of all, she sought to understand why her informants, in spontaneous narration, remained silent about lengthy periods of their lives under fascism. This 'self-censorship', she concluded, represented evidence of a psychological scar, 'a profound wound in daily experience'.[42] Passerini drew upon Freud's concept of repression, in which painful memories are defensively excluded from consciousness, to explain this collective amnesia, and she emphasized the importance of recognizing what is excluded from oral narratives about the past, as well as what is included.

Secondly, Passerini explored the ideological dimensions of workplace anecdotes and jokes in the context of contemporary Italian debates over the response of the working class to fascism. Ultimately, she suggested, such stories expressed her informants' ambivalences as they struggled to reconcile inherited beliefs with changing workplace relations under fascism. Individual subjectivity, therefore, derived from the interaction between inherited socialization and the 'capacity for self-reflection' and critique. And it is through the latter process, Passerini concluded, that 'the determinism of the cultural and psychological contents of subjectivity', could be broken.[43] In this sense, therefore Passerini shares the approach to human agency evident in the work of both Gramsci and Williams. In these memories of Italy under Mussolini, while the social environment played a critical role in shaping subjectivity, anecdotes and humour indicated the existence and potential of an individual and subversive intellectual agency.

Luisa Passerini's work profoundly influenced subsequent research in oral history. Memories of the 'subaltern' in society remained a powerful stream of research, often related to specific goals of advocacy and empowerment. But along-side these older imperatives to record oral history emerged a new theoretical engagement with the nature of the source. Much more attention began to be paid to the dimensions of individual subjectivity, and the processes of shaping an oral narrative. Oral historians began to recognize elements of narrative construction and moral rhetoric, of myth and legend. These were no longer perceived as negating the value of the life history, as empiricist historians had argued. Rather, these dimensions of the oral testimony offered the historian a unique opportunity to actively explore, through the recorded interview, the conceptual framework, values and beliefs through which all experience is, and has been, filtered and understood. In this approach to oral history 'all autobiographical memory is true; [but] it is up to the interpreter to discover in which sense, where, for which purpose'.[44] In 1979 Passerini called for new conceptual approaches that could 'succeed in drawing out their full implications', and over the last twenty years historians have begun to disentangle the cultural threads that together provide the shape and texture for the individual life narrative.[45]

## ▶ Narrative structure and 'composure'

Oral historians have paid a great deal of attention to the narrative structure of life histories, in many cases drawing upon theories from linguistics and literary studies. These analyses have generated valuable insights into the ways in which people make sense of their lives. One of the first to actively apply interdisciplinary perspectives, Ronald Grele drew upon concepts deriving from contemporary debates within structural linguistics.[46] Analysing interviews carefully, he argued, enabled oral historians to 'grasp the deeper structures which organize this seemingly unorganized flow of words'.[47] Grele analysed two interviews conducted with elderly Jewish garment workers, both active unionists, in New York City.[48] The two narratives shared very similar ideological dimensions, emphasizing the strength of the garment workers' union, its earlier successes and contemporary weakness. But underlying each story lay quite different views of the historical process. The first was based upon a cyclical perception of history, a story of rise and decline. The second, however, drew its structure from 'a more dramatic view of eternally contending binary oppositions'. While Grele suggested how each testimony might have been influenced by individual experience, he concluded that there was not sufficient evidence 'to state with any clarity or precision what it is that accounts for the differences among the various ways in which the past is structured and used – how myth becomes history and history becomes myth . . . '.

Marie-Françoise Chanfrault-Duchet also argues that the defining features of a self-directed life narrative lie in the organization of the narrative, reflected through key patterns that both relate the self to the social, and give coherence to the story:

> Aiming to dramatize the self, this pattern reproduces throughout the narrative a recognizable matrix of behaviour that imposes a coherence on the speaker's life experience, the coherence of the self. This pattern most often deals with the reproduction or transgression of the hegemonic social model. . . . Speakers, in fact, attempt to express – in narrative terms – their relation to social models. In their anecdotes, they picture themselves confronted with the dominant model and always actualizing the same pattern of behaviour: identification, acceptance or at least compromise, and so on, on the one hand; defiance, refusal, exclusion, and so on, on the other. [49]

Depending upon the key pattern, individuals may utilize one or more narrative models for their story. Chanfrault-Duchet identifies three: the epic (identification with the values of the community), the romanesque (the quest for authentic values in a degraded world), and the picaresque (an ironic and satirical position in relation to hegemonic values). The choice of narrative model provides valuable insights, she suggests, into 'the complexity, the ambiguities, and even the contradictions of the relations between the subject and the world . . . '.[50]

Anecdotes, short and humorous stories about specific incidents, also reveal the tensions and contradictions experienced by the individual. These are 'frozen' stories, repeated in public contexts, which resist interruption.[51] Luisa Passerini drew attention to the moral values and judgements implicit within workplace anecdotes, and stories of resistance to authority are to be found within many working-class historical narratives.[52] In Simon Featherstone's analysis of an interview recorded with Derbyshire miner Jack Hill, the anecdotes provide an 'opportunity to trace the way in which historical value is being defined within the culture of the teller, rather than the culture of the interview'.[53] These stories revolve around dramatic conflict between the narrator, Jack Hill, and a figure of authority. The latter is usually overcome, at least in part, by Jack Hill's skill and cunning, and as such he is represented as a 'trickster hero'. The humour in these stories always carries value judgements, describing 'comic victories over specific injustices'. Featherstone emphasizes that Jack Hill recounted these stories in a variety of public contexts; these were not simply personal stories but 'already-negotiated expressions of common history, created in the context of their performance'. In stories told on social occasions in public settings, the audience plays a critical part in both production and interpretation. It is important to recognize the element of performance that is inherent in any oral history encounter. Oral histories 'are made by persons in interaction, situated in real time and space, [and] we can see that however modest the speaker's aim, they are purposeful social actions'.[54] Furthermore, the goals of the performer will only be met if both audience and narrator are capable of fully understanding one another. The key feature of genres is that they 'depend on shared rules of interpretation: they are not explicable by form alone'.[55]

Anecdotes and stories can also reveal the ways in which social or cultural values are identified and reinforced within a group. On the New Zealand waterfront, in the middle decades of the twentieth century, waterside workers acquired nicknames that often took the place of given names. The nicknames performed a double function: cementing the bonds of friendship among the men, while also putting individuals in their place. Some nicknames were quite innocuous; but others had clear moral implications, and not a few were quite cruel or censorious. One man, who frequented bars and clubs when not required for work, was known as the Drifting Drunk; other examples were the Reluctant Fish (who refused to handle a hook), or the Judge (who was always sitting on a case). These references to working habits undoubtedly had a critical edge, and suggest that nicknames were also used as a form of social critique. Many men must have been constantly reminded, albeit with humour, of disreputable incidents or individual failings. On the other hand, admired masculine characteristics were also identified: for example, a strong physique and a willingness to work hard, to pull your weight. The stories about the origins of nicknames provide insight into the workplace culture, and the ways in which camaraderie and loyalty were reinforced through humour.[56]

A final example of narrative composition comes from Alistair Thomson's study of Anzac soldiers from the First World War. [57] The key concept at the centre of Thomson's 'cultural theory of remembering' is that of 'composure'. The process of composure consists of two particular dimensions. The first is that life narratives are constructed out of the language, metaphors and meanings of culture, consistent with the approaches we have already discussed. Secondly, Thomson argues that 'composure' is an apt name for a process through which an individuals seeks to make sense of their lives, reconciling past and present to achieve a sense of composure, to feel comfortable about the past. Thomson's study illustrates both these dimensions. The memories of old Australian soldiers were profoundly influenced by the Anzac legend, represented in popular war films and public commemorations. Thomson argues that the Anzac legend, which emphasized the soldiers' bravery, camaraderie and the disrespect for authority, was a homogeneous construction closely related to masculine and national ideals and identity. For many soldiers the public narratives of the Anzac legend 'recognised key aspects of the diggers' experience, such as comradeship, endurance, personal worth and national identity, and has provided a positive affirmation of that experience. The

Anzac legend has thus helped many veterans to compose a past they can live with.' But other old soldiers retained memories that did not correspond to the legend, stories of pain or fear, and these men were 'forced into alienation or silence'.[58] It was not until the Anzac legend was tempered by the war in Vietnam, a much more controversial military engagement, that the memories of some of those Thomson recorded could be publicly articulated and validated.

## ▶ Myths and legends

The role of myths and legends in shaping life stories became a central interest of oral historians in the 1980s, and an international oral history conference in 1987 focused on the theme of myth and history. Raphael Samuel defined myth as 'a metaphor for the symbolic order, or for the relationship between the imaginary and the real'.[59] Myth, conference participants agreed, is a fundamental component of human thought, and the published conference papers demonstrated the vitality of myths in oral testimonies, from 'the self-made man' to the 'wicked stepmother'. Others illustrated the capacity of myth to suppress alternative stories, especially when these challenged ideological constructs such as gender.[60] Concluding that gender was central to any understanding of the role of myth in oral history, the editors drew attention to an 'undisclosed misogyny [that] runs as a current through the universe of myth'. Heroic roles are overwhelmingly male, whereas the idealized female is passive and self-sacrificing.[61]

Nonetheless, historians in different cultural contexts have found that stories of resistance and challenge to authority appear to run through many women's life narratives. This challenge may take place in many different social forums, but at the heart of the encounter is the expression of active individual agency on the part of the narrator. Luisa Passerini identified a common theme of irreverence and rebelliousness in working-class women's oral narratives. She argued that such stories may be symbolic rather than literal, 'the means of expressing problems of identity in the context of a social order repressive of women . . . '.[62] Alessandro Portelli has compared the prevalence of war stories within male narratives with stories about health and hospitals by women.[63] In the latter, women stood up to and challenged the medical hierarchies, which they regarded as negligent or highhanded. In New Zealand Jane Moodie recorded the memories of families who won postwar government ballots for undeveloped farming land. The men's narratives pivoted around the heroic pioneer legend, but the women were ambivalent about their supporting roles, and 'told stories of defiance and rebellion, of asserting their independence by transgressing womanly roles in different ways'.[64]

But myth is not always a repressive force, and in some cases may provide a framework through which those experiencing radical change can reconcile past and present. In the 1970s Julie Cruikshank recorded the life histories of eight Yukon women of Athapaskan and Tlingit ancestry.[65] All were born around the time of the gold-rush of 1896–8, a period which initiated fundamental disruptive change to the Yukon Indians' economy and social organization. Cruikshank's goal was 'to document perspectives on northern social history', but her approach was consciously subverted by those she recorded, who insisted upon utilizing 'traditional oral narrative as an explanation of their individual life experiences'. Many of the women's stories revolved around the theme of the stolen woman, who:

> is taken to an unfamiliar world. Instead of acquiring an animal helper as a man would, the woman focuses her mental energies on actively escaping back to the human community. In most stories, she manages to outwit her captors and to escape on her own, often actually assisting would-be rescuers. It is her powers of reasoning rather than supernatural assistance which save her. She relies on what she has been taught at puberty about dealing with supernatural power to think her way out of her dilemma.[66]

Cruikshank concludes that 'elderly Athapaskan storytellers are using old narrative forms to think about new social problems'. In this context, the traditional stories provided a positive cultural resource for thinking about contemporary problems in the present, as well as the past.

## ▶ Cultural scripts and discourse

So far we have examined oral history research that supports many of Bartlett's and Halbwachs's original insights. Remembering is an active process of construction, one in which the individual draws upon linguistic forms and cultural beliefs to construct a more or less coherent narrative, shaped by the social context within which the story is told. Some cultural historians have taken this a step further, fitting individual narratives to public cultural scripts or discourses. An example of this approach may be found in Penny Summerfield's poststructuralist analysis of women's Second World War oral narratives, *Reconstructing Women's Wartime Lives* (1998). In this study, Summerfield explores the way women's oral histories relate to publicly available representations and discourses about women's lives during this period. Each chapter begins with a summary of the relevant public pre-war discourses, such as the daughter/filial relationship. These are gleaned from a variety of sources, such as official government policies, girls' magazines, and films. The oral histories recorded with women who lived through the war are then located within the matrix of these publicly available discourses. It could be argued that the results are reductionist, and complex answers are forced into the categories of, for example, 'stoic' or 'heroic' narratives. It is difficult to understand, in the poststructuralist model adopted by Summerfield, why individuals adopt a specific perspective, or how changes in individual perception could occur. Rather than exploring how and why ideas, values and beliefs are critiqued, reassembled, juxtaposed or rejected, her focus appears to be on how far the oral narratives fit pre-existing cultural frameworks.

Other oral historians have found that a narration that seemingly draws upon a conventional cultural 'script' or discourse may be more subversive than is first apparent. For example, in an oral history interview with an 'ordinary' Italian American housewife, an interviewee almost 'effaced' herself in the initial spontaneous narrative, submerging herself within a conventional family story. But an insightful analysis focusing upon how the words 'but' and 'just' were used within the narrative revealed the ways in which the interviewee mediated the gender constraints and expectations of her life:

> As the first audience for Mrs F.'s text, and later one of her reader interpreters, I came to stand before it not with an authority over its interpretation that would foreclose or exhaust its multiple meanings, but with a certain humility, admiration, and, eventually sympathy. For me the ingenuity (*not* ingenuousness or disingenuousness) of Mrs F.'s narrative is the way in which it allows for, but also contains, a multiplicity of positions that are contradictory, yet also permits a certain fluidity of identity within the constraints of her gender, ethnicity, and class.[67]

The social functionalism and determinism evident in both Bartlett and Halbwachs has, therefore, been challenged. Oppositional memories are retained, and surface when the environment is more conducive to their narration. Women's memories are not exclusively shaped by their prescribed social roles. Anecdotes may turn hierarchies upside down. There is little room for choice or the active agency of a conscious human being in the work of the early theorists, and Halbwachs's model does not allow for social change.[68] How do we explain why individuals choose one narrative model over another, or tell parodic anecdotes? Furthermore, when Halbwachs's subsumes individual memories under the rubric of 'collective' memory it is misleading:

> there is no single undifferentiated collectivity which is 'the social' . . . Rather than holism, the hallmark of 'the social' is discontinuity, and no two people will have identical lives. Cognitively, the recognition of dislocation and difference is built into us all, and we are all creatures of choice.[69]

The exercise of choice and moral agency is a central theme in individual life narratives. Without it, some have argued, there is no life story. What happens to the life narrative when the individual has lived through traumatic experiences in which their ability to control or influence their environment has been completely negated?

## ▶ Trauma and remembering

The largest archives of human memory have been compiled from recorded interviews with survivors of the Shoah, or Holocaust. When, during the Second World War, the Nazi regime in Germany killed six million European Jews in an attempt to eliminate the population, both the goal and the means used to try and obtain it were unprecedented in human history. The memories of many of the survivors of the concentration camps have been recorded, in a process that began at the end of the 1970s and continues up to the present.[70] Their memories suggest that the experience of losing complete control over their lives, appalling brutality, and loss of family and community, left the survivors unable to compose, in Thomson's term, life narratives that reconcile past and present. In Lawrence Langer's exceptional study *Holocaust Testimonies: The Ruins of Memory*, the experience of losing the ability to exercise moral agency in an environment where the will to survive cancelled out other human imperatives left survivors with anguished, humiliated, tainted and unheroic memories. These memories prevented 'the evolution of an integrated vision' of either the individual self or the whole life. The survivors also struggled to find the words to express the horror of what they had witnessed or experienced. Yet they persisted in telling stories that, in some cases, their families and the interviewers found too painful to hear, actively seeking to stop the interview or change the subject. The inability to exercise either control or moral agency, and prevent the loss of family and community, were central to both the content and form of the survivors' memories. Nor should we assume, Langer suggests, that these kinds of challenges 'to personhood in the twentieth century must be confined to this particular atrocity alone':

> History inflicts wounds on individual moral identity that are untraceable to personal choice or qualitative frameworks – though the scars they leave are real enough, reminding us that theoretical hopes for an integrated life must face the constant challenge to that unity by self-shattering events like the Holocaust experience.[71]

## ▶ Conclusion

Remembering, therefore, is an active process of seeking to make sense of the past, an 'effort after meaning', as Frederic Bartlett put it.[72] Central to every life narrative is the expression of values and beliefs. When these come into conflict with experience as they did, for example, with some Anzac soldiers, or the survivors of the Shoah, then individuals struggle to compose a narrative that reconciles past and present, or presents a coherent sense of self. Oral testimonies provide cultural historians with insights into this relationship between the material world and social relations on one hand, and the subjective, cultural world of individuals on the other.

The oral historian Alessandro Portelli perceives facilitating the relationship between individual memory and public understandings of history as his primary task. Individual memories, he suggests, provide links between the grand narratives of history and personal experience; he seeks to 'connect [memories] with "history" and in turn force history to listen to them'.[73] Why is it important for history to listen to memory? The murderous record of twentieth-century world history is, perhaps, one good reason. As Mirek, in Milan Kundera's novel *The Book of Laughter and Forgetting*, tells his friends, 'The struggle of man against power is the struggle of memory against forgetting.'[74] The next chapter continues with the theme of memory, and examines the contested concepts and processes surrounding the production of public, collective memory.

# 6 Collective Memory

In the last two decades cultural historians have turned their attention to the formation of popular historical consciousness, and debated whether there is such a phenomenon as 'collective memory'. In part, this is a response to what has been described as a popular 'memory boom of unprecedented proportions'.[1] The evidence of the 'obsession with memory' was evident everywhere, German cultural critic Andreas Huyssen argued in the mid-1990s, from the expansion of museums, building of new monuments and restoration of historic neighbourhoods, to retro fashions, film and television. He concluded that 'a museal sensibility seems to be occupying ever larger chunks of everyday culture and experience'.[2] In many different cultural contexts, the past acquired a new popularity through both elite and popular cultural forms and activities.

At the same time, it was argued, theories of history failed to recognize the significance of these developments, largely ignoring the multiplicity of sites where history was 'produced'.[3] Over the last decade historians have sought to address this lacuna, and there is now a substantial body of work investigating these multiple 'sites of memory', and addressing the relationship between memory and history.[4] Gaps in our understanding remain. Despite the influence of the visual media in shaping perceptions of the past, critical analysis of film and television is comparatively recent.[5] As the film historian Robert Rosenstone concluded:

> all this activity has hardly led to a consensus on how to evaluate the contribution of the 'historical' film to 'historical understanding'. Nobody has yet begun to think systematically about what Hayden White has dubbed *historiophoty* – 'the representation of history and our thought about it in visual images and filmic discourse'.[6]

A more developed and complex body of cultural history has concentrated upon the 'materiality of memory': the construction, preservation or interpretation of heritage sites, monuments and museum exhibitions, and this chapter will focus primarily upon this literature.[7]

Many of the studies exploring memory and history have also addressed broader questions: have human societies always remembered the past in the same way?

Why are contemporary Western societies so preoccupied with memory? Is there a history of memory? What is the relationship between the rise of the nation-state and collective memory, and between individual memory and collective memory? And in what ways have new technologies changed the nature of collective memory? We will refer to these questions at various points throughout the chapter, but let us begin with three pioneering texts, from the 1980s, that sought to outline the dimensions of the 'memory boom' and consider the implications for history, collective memory and heritage.

## ▶ The 'memory boom'

In 1985 David Lowenthal's study of heritage – drawing on examples primarily from Britain and the United States – was widely influential in opening up the debates over heritage, memory, and history. 'To an American', he wrote, 'the landscape of the 1980s seems saturated with "creeping heritage".' By heritage, Lowenthal meant physical artefacts, landscapes and buildings, as well as historical re-enactments and commemorations. The title of his book, *The Past is a Foreign Country*, was taken from the novel *The Go-Between* by L. P. Hartley, and reflected the central argument he wished to make. The preoccupation with identification, protection and display of historical artefacts, he suggested, prevents recognition of a central feature of our relationship with the past. The first dimension of this relationship is the foreign-ness of the past. 'However faithfully we preserve, however authentically we restore, however deeply we immerse ourselves in bygone times', Lowenthal writes, 'life back then was based on ways of being and believing incommensurable with our own.' Consequently, the 'past conjured up is . . . largely an artefact of the present'.[8]

This leads us to Lowenthal's second point. Given the unknowable nature of the past, rather than continually seek some kind of frozen historical authenticity (which is impossible) Lowenthal suggested a living, interactive relationship with the past, 'one which fuses past with present'. As an example, he described attempts to preserve a key landscape from the 1770s American War of Independence:

> The managed past may end up not merely segregated but unwittingly destroyed. In Massachusetts, for example, the Concord–Lexington 1775 combat route was set aside for the Minute Man National Historical Park in the 1960s. To display the story of that day, residents were evicted, post-Revolutionary houses demolished, and traditional farming brought to an end. The remaining houses were boarded up, fields and pastures reverted to brush, and within a few years the whole countryside ceased to bear any resemblance to the Revolutionary epoch's usage. Instead of a living landscape with past and present visibly and functionally linked, a

sumptuous visitor centre now shows surrogate relics and events of 1775 in audio-vision; outdoors, where the skirmishes actually happened, elaborate notices along a measured, wood-chipped trail interpret the historical views that could have been seen before the National Park Service obliterated them.

Lowenthal concluded that we 'should not deceive ourselves that we can keep the past stable and segregated. . . . Only by altering and adding to what we save does our heritage remain real, alive, and comprehensible.'[9]

Raphael Samuel also considered the 'historicist turn in national life' and his compendium included the conservation of historic landmarks and the 'creation of imaginary ones – Tudor gardens, Victorian steam fairs, Edwardian shopping streets'. [10] But he saw these diverse activities in positive terms, as a reflection of a pluralist and democratic approach to the past.[11] Samuel rejected three specific critiques of these popular expressions of historical sensibility. First of all, he was scornful about academic disdain. While accepting that 'living history' was present-minded, and blurred the boundary between fact and fiction, he argued that it was:

> a good deal less megalomaniac than the idea of 'scientific' history ... It was much more attentive to the small details of everyday life . . . [and] as a mobilizing cry, 'living history' has galvanized a far greater enthusiasm than those 'new' histories which periodically make a small stir in the graduate seminars and then disappear from view.[12]

Nor did Samuel agree that the passion for conservation represented a form of 'reactionary chic . . . the triumph of aristocratic and reactionary nostalgia over the levelling tendencies of the welfare state'. This perspective tended to suggest that the past acquired hegemonic meaning, a 'closed story. . . . Politics, culture and economics are all of a piece, reinforcing one another's influence, reciprocating one another's effects.' In contrast, heritage incorporated a wide range of sources and perspectives not easily subsumed under one ideology or national narrative, although Samuel acknowledged that, as a whole, heritage could represent a search for a sense of the 'indigenous'. It is, he argued, an alternative to the present, 'heritage is more typically defined in terms of relics under threat. . . . Dissevered from any idea of national destiny, it is free to wander at will . . . .'[13]

In the same decade as Lowenthal and Samuel, Pierre Nora set out to construct an alternative 'narrative' of French national history, one based upon a thematic approach to symbolic memory. *Lieux de Mémoire* was progessively published in seven volumes between 1981 and 1992; of the original 132 essays only one-third have been translated into English and reorganized into the three-volume *Realms of Memory*.[14] The authors focus upon 'the "memory places" of French national identity as they have been constructed since the Middle Ages', and the volumes include essays about literary texts, school textbooks, buildings, food, ideologies, founding peoples, religion, symbols (for example, the Gallic Cock) and concepts (such as Liberty, Equality, Fraternity).

Nora coined the term *lieux de mémoire*, or sites of memory, which he defined as follows:

> If the expression *lieu de mémoire* must have an official definition, it should be this: a *lieu de mémoire* is any significant entity, whether material or non-material in nature, which by dint of human will or the work of time has become a symbolic element of the memorial heritage of any community....

These sites, Nora suggested, 'crystallized' the collective heritage in which French collective memory was 'rooted'.[15] But Nora argued that the sites of memory acquired memorial significance only when the society had undergone a form of rupture with the past: 'the less memory is experienced from the inside the more it exists only through its exterior scaffolding and outward signs'.[16] Nora's lamentation over the loss of interiorized, unified memory has been described as a form of 'cultural melancholia'.[17]

However, Nora does not suggest that French national identity is a fixed phenomenon. Negotiating present-day relationships with the symbolic forces of the past means that 'a realm of memory is a polyreferential entity that can draw on a multiplicity of cultural myths that are appropriated for different ideological or political purposes.'[18] Nora seeks to make a distinction between his form of symbolic, multivocal, 'imagined community', and orthodox, empirical, linear national history. As he remarks, *Realms of Memory* seeks to 'decompose that unity, to dismantle its chronological and teleological continuity'.[19] But this leads us to the exclusions from Nora's symbolic framework of collective memory. *Realms of Memory* reflects the traditional focus of historians, with reliance upon archival sources and the records of the elite. In Nora's conceptualization of French collective memory, it has been argued, the impact of empire is ignored, regional and local perspectives neglected, and the role of gender in shaping collective memory absent.[20] In this sense, Nora's approach to collective memory is centrist and top–down compared with that of Raphael Samuel, which is from the margin and from below.

These three texts, by Lowenthal, Samuel and Nora, documented the extent of the 'memory boom' and suggested a cultural paradox. In the rapidly changing world of the last half of the twentieth century, connections that made memory meaningful as a means of explaining the present had been severed, but at the same time individuals and societies turned to their material heritage to construct their own senses of indigenousness and narrative continuity. However, while all three authors addressed the issue of memory in contemporary society, the overall picture appeared quite anarchic and fragmented. To what extent do *lieux de mémoire* and heritage reflect 'collective memory'? To better understand the theoretical underpinnings of subsequent studies of historical memory, we must first consider four key concepts that are central to this historiography: memory, collective memory, identity and heritage.

## ▶ Memory

Cultural historians have applied the concept of memory to both the individual recall of direct experience, and how social groups – both large and small – remember aspects of the past they have not witnessed or experienced. This is the crux of the problem around the contemporary use of the term: it is used to describe two rather different ways of knowing. As Samuel Hynes, historian of the First World War and veteran of the Second World War, argued:

> The problem is the word *memory* itself. It is common for historians who write about memorials to say that memorials as a class embody and communicate memory; but I find it hard to see how this can possibly be true, unless, like Humpty Dumpty, we make words mean what we *say* they mean. Memory is the mental faculty by which we preserve or recover our pasts, and also the events recovered. Without that link – now reaching back to then – you have an image of the past in your mind, but it isn't memory but something else, a social construction, history.[21]

Historians seek to understand the relationship between present, past and future in human consciousness, and it is clear that this relationship has changed over time. Memory itself has a history, and the way the past is remembered, and its relationship to the present and the future, are not fixed.[22] A schematic outline of collective European attitudes towards the past, present and future would reflect these changing perspectives:

> in pagan antiquity, the valorization of the past predominated along with the idea of a decadent present; in the Middle Ages, the present is trapped between the weight of the past and the hope of an eschatological future; in the Renaissance, on the contrary, the primary stress is on the present, while from the seventeenth to the nineteenth centuries, the ideology of progress turns the valorization of time towards the future.[23]

What about memory at the beginning of the twenty-first century? Is it possible to characterize the contemporary relationship between present, past and future?

Like many commentators, Andreas Huyssen argues that belief in human progress and optimism about the future was severely shaken by 'the [twentieth] century's political totalitarianisms, colonial enterprises, and ecological ravages'. The Holocaust, or Shoah, has dominated debates over collective memory in contemporary society, challenging 'the humanist and universalist claims of Western civilisation'. The loss of faith in an ideology of progress, Huyssen continues, led to an obsession with memory as 'a reaction formation against the accelerating technical processes that are transforming our *Lebenswelt* (lifeworld) in quite distinct ways'. Huyssen saw the memory boom as a 'healthy sign of contestation: contestation of the informational hyperspace and an expression of the basic human need to live in extended structures of temporality'. But he also believed that it embraced a 'frozen' past, a retreat from the present, rather than being oriented towards informing our actions in the future.[24] This interpretation shares some common ground with the contemporaneous studies by Lowenthal, Samuel and Nora discussed a little earlier.

## ▶ Collective memory

Many cultural historians use the term 'collective memory' when discussing the ways in which societies remember the past. The term itself is controversial, and there is no agreed-upon definition. One definition of collective memory is very open-ended: 'the representation of the past and the making of it into a shared cultural knowledge by successive generations in "vehicles of memory", such as books, films, museums, commemorations, and others'.[25] The wide scope of this definition is problematic since it allows a variety of quite different creative processes to be subsumed under the catch-all phrase of 'collective memory'. Some of the difficulties originate with the conceptualization of collective memory first articulated by Maurice Halbwachs and discussed in the previous chapter. Let us revisit briefly this original formulation of collective memory, which has shaped the contemporary terminology and debate within memory studies.

Halbwachs argued that all memory is collective memory because 'memory depends on the social environment'.[26] Individual recollections, in Halbwach's definition, do not combine to create collective memory. Rather the social environment shapes individual memories into a coherent collective memory:

> the collective frameworks of memory are not constructed after the fact by the combination of individual recollections. . . . Collective frameworks are, to the contrary, precisely the instruments used by the collective memory to reconstruct an image of the past which is in accord, in each epoch, with the predominant thoughts of the society.[27]

Halbwachs applied this model of collective memory to enduring, cohesive communities such as the family, religious societies and social classes. An individual could, therefore, contribute and subscribe to multiple collective memories, each shaped by the groups to which he or she belongs. Halbwachs also argued that these collective memories are in a constant process of modification, as they are adapted to fit contemporary needs and conceptual frameworks. It has been suggested that this theorization of memory shares common ground with Claude Lévi-Strauss's concept of *bricolage*, in that the same historical objects may be adopted for different purposes in a multiplicity of cultural contexts.[28]

Halbwachs also drew attention to the way in which place and commemoration are mnemonic devices for fixing collective memories. In a powerful essay, entitled 'The Legendary Topography of the Gospels in the Holy Land', Halbwachs described the biblical Holy Lands 'as an imaginary scheme conjured up during the Middle Ages and superimposed upon the landscape of Palestine'. From the fourth century onwards, 'European pilgrims constructed a Holy Land of physical shrines that faithfully reflected their religious conceptions of Christ's sojourn on earth. . . . Mnemonic props to a creed, the shrines of the Holy Land were also monuments to the rising power of Christianity to impose its living memories upon the space of an alien culture.'[29] Halbwachs's essay, in particular, foreshadowed much of the recent research into the relationship between memory, geographical place and material objects such as memorials and monuments.

There are two dimensions of Halbwachs's paradigm over which historians have explicitly demurred. The first concerns the relegation of individual memory to an almost invisible presence, and the second relates to the social processes through which collective memories are constructed. First of all, historians have taken issue with the absence of the thinking, *remembering* individual from Halbwachs's accounts. For example, James Young rejects the sublimation of individual memory under the rubric of 'collective memory':

> I prefer to examine 'collected memory', the many discrete memories that are gathered into common memorial spaces and assigned common meaning. A society's memory, in this context, might be regarded as an aggregate collection of its members' many, often competing memories.
>
> For even though groups share socially constructed assumptions and values that organize memory into roughly similar patterns, individuals cannot share another's memory any more than they can share another's cortex. . . . By maintaining a sense of collected memories, we remain aware of their disparate sources, of every individual's unique relation to a lived life, and of the ways our traditions and cultural forms continuously assign common meaning to disparate memories.[30]

Secondly, Halbwachs's model of 'collective memory' easily slips into the reification of memory, and neglects the complex processes of negotiation, contestation and reception involved in the construction of shared memories. In the last ten years or so, cultural historians have paid more attention to the specific social and cultural processes through which collective memories are created (although perhaps less to how they are received). This is reflected in the tripartite model of collective memory proposed by Wulf Kansteiner:

> the result of the interaction among three types of historical factors: the intellectual and cultural traditions that frame all our representations of the past, the memory makers who selectively adopt and manipulate these traditions, and the memory consumers who use, ignore, or transform such artifacts according to their own interests.'[31]

A recent collection of essays by historical sociologists reached similar conclusions, but defined collective memory as the process, rather than the end result. Describing 'social remembering' as the 'ideological projects and practices of actors in settings', the sociologists emphasized the processual and contested nature of memory, and preferred 'mnemonic practices' to the reductive and reified concept of collective memory.[32]

Within the small sample of writings above, we find historians and historical sociologists replacing 'collective memory' with other terms, for example, 'collected memories' and 'mnemonic practices'. During the chapter this list will expand to include 'cultural memory', 'imagined communities', 'invented traditions', 'theatres of memory', 'sites of memory', 'mnemonic communities', 'social remembering', 'collective remembrance' and 'public memory'. Each of these phrases qualifies Halbwachs's formulation of 'collective memory' in a particular way, and together they reflect an emphasis upon pluralism, process, power, agency and medium of communication by contemporary scholars engaged in the study of how societies collectively remember the past.

## ▶ Identity and heritage

It is widely accepted that memory is central to the construction of both individual and collective identities, for example those adopted by religious, ethnic or national groups.[33] Material objects or places can play a critical mnemonic role in reinforcing and perpetuating collective identities, and therefore heritage in the form of 'objectivised culture . . . texts, images, rites, buildings, monuments, cities, or even landscapes', act as the 'concretion of identity' for particular groups.[34] Heritage has, therefore, become of central importance to particular ethnic peoples and nations, a way of asserting collective uniqueness. However, such identities are not immutable, since memory and assumed identity exist in a reciprocal relationship. Those memories which best serve present needs may be utilized to construct a usable past:

> identities and memories are highly selective, inscriptive rather than descriptive, serving particular interests and ideological positions. Just as memory and identity support one another, they also sustain certain subjective positions, social boundaries, and, of course, power.[35]

The relationship between identity and heritage has been critiqued on a number of fronts. First of all, it has been argued that the adoption of Western concepts of identity and heritage result in the commodification of material culture and objects of symbolic value.[36] Secondly, our attention has also been drawn to the role of nostalgia in heritage. Heritage is often drained of uncomfortable meanings, and incites pride rather than guilt.[37] This is one reason why there is an uneasy relationship between historians and heritage. It has been argued that historians may 'embellish, or be co-opted' by heritage, but that history and heritage are not identical:

> This is the crux of what distinguishes heritage from history. To serve as a collective symbol heritage must be widely accepted by insiders, yet inaccessible to outsiders. Its data are social, not scientific. Socially binding traditions must be accepted on faith, not by reasoning. Heritage thus defies empirical analysis; it features fantasy, invention, mystery, error.[38]

Memory, collective memory, identity and heritage exist in close and reciprocal relationships. Consequently, in a world organized largely through nation-states and suffering from the bloodiest century of conflict, much recent work has focused on the relationship between memory and nationalism. The use of collective memory by elites to legitimate teleological ideas of national origin and descent has a long history.[39] As Eric Hobsbawm pungently commented some time ago, 'historians are to nationalism what poppy-growers in Pakistan are to heroin-addicts: we supply the essential raw material for the market'.[40] Following the critical work on **nationalism** by Hobsbawm and others, many historians now approach national collective traditions and memories with more circumspection. Many conflicts of the twentieth century have been undertaken in the name of ethnic or religious identity and memory. Given that 'it is estimated that among the existing 185 sovereign states, few are ethnically homogeneous while around 40 per cent contain five or more ethnic groups', better understanding of the relationship between collective memory and nationalism is a critical task.[41] It is essential that historians 'study the reifications of nationalists without certifying them ontologically'.[42]

## ▶ 'Imagined communities' and invented traditions

In seeking to understand the rise and spread of nationalism, historians have turned to the role of culture, and cultural **symbols**, in their attempt to unearth its enduring appeal. In 1983 Benedict Anderson published his path-breaking study of the growth of nationalism, which profoundly influenced the direction of subsequent studies. 'My point of departure', Anderson began, 'is that nationality, or, as one might prefer to put it in view of that word's multiple significations, nationness, as well as nationalism, are cultural artefacts of a particular kind.' Anderson's definition of a nation contains the key concept for which he is best known. The nation 'is an *imagined political community* . . . imagined because the members of even the smallest nation will never know most of their fellow members, meet them, or even hear of them, yet in the minds of each lives the image of their communion'.[43]

The cultural roots of nationalism, Anderson argued, lay within a particular historical matrix towards the end of the eighteenth century when 'three fundamental cultural conceptions, all of great antiquity, lost their axiomatic grip of men's minds'. These three conceptions were: 'the idea that a particular script-language offered privileged access to ontological truth' (for example, Latin); the divinely-ordained nature of a hierarchical society; and the understanding of time 'in which cosmology and history were indistinguishable'. The decline in these certainties, following economic change and scientific discoveries, created the climate for 'a new way of linking fraternity, power and time meaningfully together'. Nationalism emerged as the new integrative concept, but in a form profoundly influenced by the earlier conceptual preoccupations. And in its name millions were to willingly give their lives over the next two centuries. What, Anderson asks, can possibly explain such 'colossal sacrifices'?[44]

First of all, Anderson argues that key preoccupations of religious thought, such as the 'attempt to find meaning in human suffering and mortality', were transferred into the secular imagination of the nation. The image of the Tomb of the Unknown Soldier is 'saturated with ghostly *national* imaginings', in particular linking death and nationalism. In an effective comparison, Anderson argues that the 'cultural significance of such monuments becomes even clearer if one tries to imagine, say, a Tomb of the Unknown Marxist, or a cenotaph for fallen Liberals'. Secondly, while nation-states are new in terms of history, nations are always presented as old, 'always loom out of an immemorial past, and, still more important, glide into a limitless future'. Anderson points to the nineteenth-century colonial enterprises of census, map and museum, and how the latter in particular, along with monuments and archaeological sites, provided the 'legitimacy of its [the nation's] ancestry'.[45]

A set of essays edited by Eric Hobsbawm and Terence Ranger, and published the same year, followed a parallel argument to that of Anderson. *The Invention of Tradition* emphasized the construction of fictitious historical links with the past as 'a legitimator of action and cement of group cohesion'. Invented tradition is defined as:

> a set of practices, normally governed by overtly or tacitly accepted rules and of a ritual or symbolic nature, which seek to inculcate certain values and norms of behaviour by repetition, which automatically implies continuity with the past. In fact, where possible, they normally attempt to establish continuity with a suitable historic past. [46]

The most widely cited chapter in the book, by Hugh Trevor-Roper, is an entertaining and ironic debunking of the kilt as a symbol of ancient Scots national identity. It appears the kilt was largely invented by an astute English Quaker businessman in the second quarter of the eighteenth century, and that clan tartans emerged a little later with the formation, by the British government, of Highland regiments to fight imperial wars.[47] Hobsbawm describes invented traditions such as these as central to the modern construction and 'social engineering' of national claims and identity.[48] '[T]he state linked both formal and informal, official and unofficial, political and social inventions of tradition', he concludes, and 'increasingly defined the largest stage on which the crucial activities determining human lives as subjects and citizens were played out.'[49]

There are, however, those who see the relationship between cultural symbols and nationalism in less critical terms. Employing an 'ethno-symbolic approach', Anthony Smith emphasizes the 'central role of myths, memories, symbols, and traditions' in nationalism. As a consequence, he takes issue with three dimensions of '"imagined communities" and "invented traditions": nationalism as *invented*, in the *present*, by the *elite*'. Smith wanted to counteract 'the blocking presentism, and constructionism of much current work on ethnicity, which views our understanding of the ethnic past as social construction based on present needs and reflecting the interests and preoccupations of present generations'. Such arguments, he suggests, cannot explain the enduring appeal of nationalism.[50]

Smith argues that the fundamental roots of nationalism lie in its 'deep' cultural resources, defined as: 'shared memories of a rich ethno-history, and especially of golden ages; religious beliefs in ethnic election, and especially sacred convenants;

and sentiments of belonging to ancestral homelands, especially sacred territories'. These resources are, nonetheless, dependent upon the 'rise of an intelligentsia, able to translate ethno-historical traditions, ethnic beliefs and territorial attachments into the language of modern nationalism'. In this argument, the premodern roots of nationalism, the 'myths, memories, traditions, and symbols of ethnic heritages' are embedded in popular consciousness. Elites may reconstitute these 'deep cultural resources' in each generation, but must still 'adhere to the cultural patterns and remain within the cultural parameters laid down by successive generations of a particular ethno-history'.[51] To what extent does Smith verge on ontologically certifying the ideological reification of memory? The two historians that follow explicitly question the historical validity of 'ethno-history' in framing contemporary collective memory.

Yael Zerubavel's analysis of the making of Israeli collective memory illustrates the close relationship between present and past, between the goals of a political movement and representations of the past. Zerubavel focuses upon the changing interpretations of three specific memory sites that 'did not occupy a major place in traditional Jewish memory yet emerged as major turning points in the master commemorative narrative of Israeli society'. One of the three memory sites is the ancient fortress of Masada. In AD 73 the Jewish defenders of the fortress, according to the single account by Josephus, a Jewish historian and commander of the Jewish army in Galilee, elected to 'kill themselves so as to die as free people rather than be enslaved by the Romans'. The story of Masada did not, however, 'play a major role in Jewish collective memory' until it attracted the attention of Zionist scholars in the nineteenth century. During the subsequent century Masada became a major commemorative site, with enthusiastic state sponsorship. There is no doubting, Zerubavel comments, 'Masada's potency as a symbolic event that provides modern Israeli society with a source of legitimation from the past and a model for the future'. While multiple interpretative meanings emerged, including the secular and religious, national and archaeological, critics argue that the dominant Zionist narrative of Masada as 'a key turning point and a historical metaphor of fighting to the bitter end' has detrimentally shaped contemporary Israeli attitudes and policymaking.[52]

In a second example, Patrick Geary explores the production of national identity in Europe. Geary locates the rise of contemporary European ethnic nationalism and racist violence within the context of political fears of waves of migration, 'barbarian hordes', from the disintegrating and volatile East. In these ethnic nationalist discourses claims to identity are based upon a moment of 'primary acquisition, the first century for the Germans, the fifth for the Franks, the sixth and seventh centuries for the Croats, the ninth and tenth for the Hungarians, and so on . . . '. But Geary argues that 'there is nothing particularly ancient about either the peoples of Europe or their supposed right to political autonomy'.[53] The origins of these national narratives, Geary suggests, lie in nineteenth-century thought which drew upon the romantic political philosophies of Rousseau and Hegel, the scientific history of von Ranke, and philology, the study of languages. Regarding this as a particularly toxic brew, one that 'has destroyed Europe twice and may do so yet again', Geary concludes (in terms highly reminiscent of David Lowenthal):

> But in spite of the emotional appeal of these historical and linguistic claims, nothing in the historical record justifies them. Congruence between early medieval and contemporary 'peoples' is a myth. . . . Both in large, hegemonic states and in aspiring independence movements, claims that 'we have always been a people' actually are appeals to *become* a people – appeals not grounded in history but, rather, in attempts to create history. The past, as has often been said, is a foreign country, and we will never find ourselves there.[54]

The remembrance of war and conflict is a key dimension of national consciousness. As Raphael Samuel reminded us, 'the romanticization of war might also be considered a cultural universal . . . [entering] into the very marrow of the national idea'.[55] Anderson drew our attention earlier in the chapter to the Tomb of the Unknown Soldier, 'saturated with ghostly *national* imaginings'. A significant body of cultural history has examined war commemoration, although some of these studies, it is argued, suffer from their exclusive national focus. Jay Winter argues that a comparative approach to First World War memorialization enabled him to discover 'striking convergences in the experience of loss and the search for meaning in all combatant countries'.[56] This body of work on war memorialization and commemoration provides an excellent case study to test Kansteiner's three-dimensional model of collective memory: the intellectual and cultural frameworks, the agency of individuals and groups in memorial activities, and the interpretation and understandings of those who engage in commemorative activities.

## ▶ 'The language of mourning'

Historians have debated twentieth-century European 'language of mourning', to use Jay Winter's phrase, paying particular attention to the representation of both world wars in memorials and commemorative sites. During and after the First World War, a new language of 'truth-telling' about the war, based upon combatant experience, flourished in literature and film. In *The Great War and Modern Memory*, Paul Fussell explored the dominance of irony in memoirs and literary texts written during and after the war.[57] This 'modern memory' emphasized that 'dislocation, paradox and the ironic, could express anger and despair'. It contrasted with older, traditional languages of commemoration that emphasized glory, sacrifice, and patriotism. Winter suggests that the search for 'an appropriate language of loss' following the First World War drew more upon the traditional symbols and images that helped the bereaved to come to terms with their loss and leave the past behind.[58]

Memorials exemplify this argument. While 'the languages, imagery, and icons adopted varied considerably according to artistic convention, religious practice, and political conviction', many presented the war 'as *both* noble and uplifting *and* tragic and unendurably sad'. Many included religious figures or symbols, which suggested 'aesthetic redemption of the suffering of war, of resurrection, of transcendence'. In contrast, perhaps, in the faces of the soldiers on memorials, 'fatigue, and a reflective acceptance of duty and fate are etched into their features'. Above all, Winter argues, these memorials were built 'as places where people could mourn. And be seen to mourn . . . communal commemorative art provided first and foremost a framework for and legitimation of individual and family grief.'[59]

The Second World War, however, provided a much sharper break in the language of mourning and memory, following the loss of 'optimism and faith in human nature' upon which the earlier symbolic forms rested. Many of the new cultural forms commemorating the Second World War did not draw upon the cultural references of the earlier memorials, and were simple, austere, and abstract in form. As Julia Kristeva wrote, 'never has a cataclysm been more apocalyptically outrageous; never has its representations been assumed by so few symbolic means'.[60] The Holocaust or Shoah presented the gravest difficulties in terms of memorial representation. As James Young has pointed out, twentieth-century artists, sculptors and architects are 'working in an era of abstract expressionism, earthworks, and conceptual art, and architects [are] answerable to postmodern and deconstructivist design'. However, abstract forms of representation do not always reflect or appeal to public taste or sentiment. Such memorials:

> often run up against a wall not only of public bewilderment but also of survivor outrage. For many survivors believe that the searing reality of their experiences demands as literal a memorial expression as possible. 'We weren't tortured and our families weren't murdered in the abstract', the survivors complain, 'it was real'. In reference to his Warsaw Ghetto Monument, for example, the sculptor Nathan Rapoport once asked plaintively, 'Could I have made a rock with a hole in it and said, 'Voilà, the heroism of the Jewish people?'[61]

One contemporary war memorial that managed to bridge this divide is the Vietnam Veterans Memorial in Washington, DC. The design of the memorial was put to an open competition, and contestants were given four instructions: first, that the design should be reflective and contemplative in character; secondly, it should harmonize with its surroundings; thirdly, it must contain the names of those who had died in the conflict or who were still missing; and finally, it should make no political statement about the war.[62] The winner was a 21-year-old female art student and Chinese American, Maya Ying Lin, whose design is regarded as a 'turning point in the history of public memory, a decisive departure from the anonymity of the Tomb of the Unknown Solder'.[63] Lin proposed that the names of those who died, in the order in which they were killed, be carved into highly reflective 'black granite panels that form a large V at a 125-degree angle and suggest the pages of an open book'. The panels gradually cut more deeply into the ground, until at the centre visitors are in 'a strangely private, buffered public space'. As Kristin Hass concludes, 'The Wall manages to capture the unlikely simultaneous experiences of reflection and burial.' While Vietnam veterans, who had raised the funds for the memorial, received the design with approval others considered it an affront to those who died in the war. It was 'more mournful than heroic'; 'an admission of defeat'; 'too abstract, too intellectual, too reflective'; 'it was not celebratory, heroic, or manly'. Despite this conservative backlash, the memorial, officially dedicated in 1982, continues to receive praise for its capacity to represent the tragedy of each individual death with 'dignity and sadness'.[64]

## ▶ 'Memory-makers'

The history of the Vietnam War Memorial provides a good example of the second dimension of collective memory, the memory-makers. John Bodnar argues that public memory is a struggle between 'official memory' and 'vernacular memory'. Official memory is the province of cultural authorities drawn from all levels of society, who are primarily concerned with the stability and continuity of social and cultural memory and institutions. Vernacular memory, on the other hand, derives from those with shared interests or experiences, such as immigrant communities or soldiers. Their perspectives are often local and particular, reflecting specific social realities. While individuals may subscribe to aspects of both official and vernacular memory, Bodnar believes that the key issues for public memory is the extent to which vernacular memory can control and contain the 'cultural offensive' of official memory.[65]

The Vietnam Memorial, as Hass points out, is 'in many ways a place of contest between the vernacular memory and official memory', one in which vernacular memory largely triumphed. The movement to create a memorial was begun by a single Vietnam veteran, who with a few friends formed the Vietnam Veterans Memorial Fund (VVMF) in 1979. The men and women who formed the core of the VVMF were not from the political elite, nor were they politically or socially unified. But they did agree that they wanted 'a *veterans* memorial not a *war* memorial: the former would ensure a memory that emphasized the contributions of the soldiers rather than the federal government'. Therefore they chose to raise the necessary money through public subscription, rather than seek federal funds. Following the backlash against Maya Lin's design, intervention from the political elite led to the addition of a figurative sculpture of three soldiers, 'strong, highly masculinized, and heroic'. Nonetheless it is Maya Lin's Wall that continues to be the main focus and attraction of the memorial site. [66]

In his study of memorialization and commemoration of the First World War, Winter identifies the importance of the purposeful actions of individuals and local communities in relation to the process of memorialization. It was the middle tier of civil society that contributed most as the memory-makers for this war: 'individuals and social groups who come together, not at the behest of the state or any of its subsidiary organizations, but because they have to speak out'. Winter insists 'upon the significance of agency in the work of remembrance of particular groups of survivors, whose bond is social and experiential'.[67] The driving force is existential: the need to mourn. Other historians have questioned whether it is possible to separate the motives and actions of these agents of civil society from the politics of the state quite so neatly. They argue that it is not possible to separate the activities of civil society so easily from those of the state.[68]

Eventually, however, memories pass from direct remembrance to 'cultural memory', or 'postmemory'. The latter term signals 'the shift from narrative based on direct memory to cultural productions which explore what it means to live under the shadow of past wars'.[69] The transmission, and subsequent re-interpretation, of memories between living generations may be fraught with conflict. The tensions surrounding this shift were epitomized in the *Enola Gay* controversy. Museums are frequently the sites of contested versions of the past, as the Smithsonian museum in the United States discovered to its cost. In 1991 the National Air and Space Mmuseum (NASM) began planning an exhibition around the B-29 bomber *Enola Gay*, on the 50th anniversary of dropping the nuclear bomb on Hiroshima, Japan. The museum staff planned to place the event within a broad context, utilizing new scholarship on the war, and reflecting the impact upon the city and its peoples as well as upon American veterans from the Pacific theatre. The proposed exhibition unleashed a torrent of criticism, particularly from Second World War veterans. Objections were based upon the perceived negation of the combatants' memories and perspectives by a younger generation of historians, whose access to newly declassified documents led to a more complex and critical evaluation of the decision to drop the nuclear bomb. Following an impassioned letter from some members of the House of Representatives, claiming that this was 'one of the most morally unambiguous events of the 20th century', the NASM eviscerated the exhibition, until little remained but the shell of the aircraft itself.[70]

## ▶ 'Memory consumers'

Let us turn finally to the third leg of Kansteiner's model of collective memory, the memory consumers. Historians are now starting to look at the way in which individuals participating in the memorial culture construct their frameworks of meaning. James Young drew our attention to the 'fundamentally interactive, dialogical quality of every memorial space'.[71] But his comprehensive study of Holocaust memorials did not develop this insight. It has been argued that neither state-centred nor social agency approaches adequately explain how and why particular commemorative activities or monuments acquire purchase upon the individual mind. One way this is achieved is through the use of pre-existing cultural templates that trigger emotional identification:

> part of their subjective hold may lie in the way in which, in the remembrance of one war, they draw upon key 'pre-memories' or 'templates'. These templates, consisting of cultural narratives, myths and tropes, are the frames through which later conflicts are understood. . . . Their efficacy lies in the fact that they circulate in cultural spaces which antecede, and thus are part of the constitution of personal memory. Where subjectivities have been shaped by such templates, people *feel* the significance of these past events to be deeply personal.[72]

What happens, however, when the traditional cultural template of war memory is fractured? Following the dedication of the Vietnam Veterans Memorial in 1982, visitors began leaving diverse objects at the base of the wall, including 'photographs, medals, letters, clothing, and teddy bears'. These objects are collected by Park Service staff, then recorded and preserved in a vast warehouse. By 1993 the collection included more than 250,00 objects of all kinds. Hass argues that 'such memorial impulses reflect both the need to negotiate the public meanings of these deaths and a determination on the part of ordinary citizens to do this work themselves'. She explicitly rejects any suggestion that 'the nation is no longer the site or frame of memory for most people'.[73] On the contrary, she believes that:

> the liminal, contested place of the Vietnam War in American culture has disrupted the expectation that dead soldiers can be retired to a stoic, martyred memory of heroism and sacrifice, and in so doing, has disrupted American memorial practices. I see the gifts Americans bring to the Wall as part of a continuing public negotiation about patriotism and nationalism. These gifts forge a new mode of public commemoration that suggests ordinary Americans deeply crave a memory, or a thousand memories together, that speaks to ways in which this war disrupted their sense of American culture and their place in it.'[74]

The desire for active engagement with the past is also evident in Roy Rosenzweig and David Thelen's study of 'popular historymaking'. Americans were asked, in a wide-ranging telephone survey, about the ways in which they connected to the past, and revealed widespread active engagement through family histories, hobbies, and museum visits. All interviewees, regardless of ethnic group, placed the greatest trust in first-hand, eye-witness accounts (particularly by family members) or authentic artefacts. Television, film and books rated lowest in terms of historical truthworthiness, on the basis that these were constructed for profit, or reflected political agendas. After family histories, museums and historic sites were the most trusted sources for exploring the past.[75] Above all, respondents sought to use the past to engage with contemporary problems and issues in their lives. As Rosenzweig commented, the people they interviewed 'valued the past as a way of answering questions about identity, immortality, and responsibility. Our respondents talked at great length about the past as a source for moral guidance, but morality is not a category that has lately figured in our professional discourse, where relativist notions prevail.'[76] This study brings together individual and public memory, and provides insights into the relationship between remembering and collective forms of memorialization.

## ▶ Conclusion

Many historians would agree that the twentieth century has seen an exponential growth, in many parts of the world, in a 'memorial culture' as the 'principal avenue through which the past is interpreted'.[77] But whether this 'memorial culture' can be subsumed under 'collective memory' is another matter. As this chapter demonstrates, the unified theoretical conception implicit in the term 'collective memory' may prove to be illusory. 'Collective memory', widely used but poorly defined, should perhaps be replaced by alternative terms that better reflect its contested nature, for example 'cultural memory', which acknowledges the transition from direct to indirect memory, or 'mnemonic practices', focusing more upon the social and cultural processes of memorial construction. As James Young concluded, in the context of ongoing debate over Holocaust remembrance, 'it may also be true that the surest engagement with memory lies in its perpetual irresolution'.[78]

# Conclusion

Over the past 150 years, cultural historians have produced a rich and diverse body of work exploring the complex dimensions of human consciousness. They have drawn upon an eclectic range of theories and concepts to better understand the expression of human thought, and identified the enduring problems of cultural interpretation. Cultural historians have focused primarily upon the underlying, unconscious mental structures or patterns, the foundations of human subjectivities. In some cases these have been defined very broadly and inclusively, for example Dilthey's *Weltanschauung*, Febvre's 'mental tools', and the 'habitus' of Bourdieu. But others have also drawn upon more specific structuralist theories relating to human consciousness, ranging from the psychoanalytic to the linguistic. In more recent decades, the linguistic turn tilted cultural history decisively towards idealism, and an exclusive focus on the function of symbolic language and discourse in the codification of human consciousness. All these approaches to human subjectivity have emphasized the underlying collective psychological, social or linguistic structures or patterns that determine human thought and behaviour. At times it could appear that humanity had been assimilated into *Star Trek*'s Borg Collective and told, 'All Resistance is Futile'.

The problems with unified, coherent, and determinist approaches to culture are widely acknowledged. First, there is the too-ready assumption of cultural cohesion. If culture is a system of symbols and meanings, have cultural historians mistaken the appearance of cohesion for a more complex reality? Symbols, after all, are a representation of reality, and the process of representation itself contains within it ambiguities and ambivalences. As a consequence, Jack Goody argues, 'cognitive contradiction' permeates all cultures, and this in turn creates the potential for change.[1] If the representational process is shot through with communicative dissonance, can we talk about 'a culture' at all? Clearly there needs to be at least some form of 'thin' coherence for cultural historians to be able to identify and write about 'a culture'.[2] Natalie Zemon Davis has suggested a way out of this conundrum. Cultural coherence, she suggests, should be located in the fundamental disagreements within societies:

it's better to identify a period not so much in terms of the things that people deeply believe as in terms of the deep conflicts that divide people. That is, periods and cultures are held together by a deeply shared common argument or uncertainty. I think that is actually a much more helpful way of conceptualizing things than saying that a given period is held together because everybody believes in $x$.[3]

The advantage of this approach to culture is that it suggests a dynamic rather than a static view of human consciousness. It is one of the paradoxes of cultural histories that material or discursive conflict is always acknowledged in one form or another, but this has rarely been translated into explanations of cultural or conceptual transformation in the past. The concept of 'cognitive contradiction' *within* cultures provides one way forward to understand cultural change over time. Cultural transformation may also be found at the site of encounter *between* cultures. Bakhtin describes the creative cultural understandings that emerge from an active engagement with an unfamiliar culture; an engagement that involves trying to see not only 'through its eyes', but through both sets of eyes in a dialogue between cultures. He concluded that 'outsideness' was the key to human understanding.[4] Homi Bhabha draws similar conclusions, arguing that it is the experience of alterity, or 'otherness', that creates new cultural perspectives, and that 'our most enduring lessons for living and thinking' emerge from the marginalized and dispossessed.[5]

Warning against cultural approaches that deny the potential for human creative agency, Raymond Williams called for radical exploration of the relationship between language and individual 'inner' consciousness. This is a consistent, although minor, theme within cultural history and has kept alive the idea of the individual's capacity to reflect upon his or her own experience. While acknowledging the hegemonic power of the elite, Gramsci's formulation of class struggle began with self-consciousness, the critical interrogation of oneself as a product of history. His influence carried through to Raymond Williams and a generation of cultural Marxists. The technology of writing also enhanced the human capacity for reflexivity through the experience of 'bouncing thoughts between oneself and a piece of paper, which makes it easier to effect this separation and to ask questions'.[6] The recognition of the capacity for self-reflectiveness or self-reflexivity is a welcome antidote to the human automaton of much contemporary theorization within cultural history. There is an unfortunate tendency to acknowledge our need for intellectual reflexivity as cultural historians while denying the capacity to those we study.

However, the thinking, purposive historical subject has never entirely disappeared. Arguably the most admired cultural histories are those of individuals and small communities: Mennochio, Ménétra, and al-Hasan al-Wassan (who, I believe will join these ranks); the Pyrrenean village of Artigat in *The Return of Martin Guerre,* and the apprentices' workshop of *The Great Cat Massacre.* All have allowed us to see into the social and cultural worlds of the past through the eyes of curious, rebellious, purposeful men and women.[7] It is time for the rediscovery of individuality within cultural history.[8] One does not have to posit an entirely autonomous self to argue that human subjectivity is the result of a long period of social and cultural development specific to each individual. In this context, historians will need to pay attention to developments within neuroscience. Over the past two or three decades the study of the human brain has demonstrated both 'the essential unity of humans *and* our essential individuality'.[9] The 'genetically determined architecture of the brain', little different from those of our ancestors, co-exists with its fundamental plasticity.[10] Through a long period of development the neural pathways of the brain are constructed in response to experience and the environmental context. 'Nothing', the neuroscientist Steven Rose argues, 'makes sense in biology except in the context of history – and within history I include evolution, development, social, cultural and technological history.'[11]

In a nice turn of phrase, Rose argues that cognition is always tinged by emotion, and that Descartes's famous statement 'cogito ergo sum' ('I think, therefore, I am') should be replaced by 'Emotio ergo sum'.[12] However, it is only comparatively recently that the study of emotions has acquired renewed interest among historians. Peter and Carol Stearns initiated this discussion twenty years ago with their call for the study of 'collective emotional standards of a society', and coining the term 'emotionology' to define this approach, although the term has not been widely adopted.[13] The purpose of emotionology, according to the Stearns, is to understand the 'social factors that determine and delimit, either implicitly or explicitly, the manner in which emotions are expressed'. This definition excludes the subjective evidence of experience, and focuses on the social and cultural constraints and prescriptive literature surrounding the expression of emotion. The Stearns argue that historians have a great deal to contribute to the debate over emotion, and in particular tracing changing emotional values over time and in different contexts.[14]

But the history of emotions continues to face the old problems, including the lack of certainty among psychologists concerning the nature and expressive features of discrete emotions. Do historians have to decide whether emotions are an involuntary, biological phenomenon, or social and cultural constructions? Some cultural psychologists, anthropologists and linguists argue that rather than being inchoate mental feelings, beyond our control, emotions are culturally and socially derived. In this constructivist perspective, emotions are a learned response, in terms of both experience and expression. However, recent studies suggest that a choice does not have to be made between the biological and constructivist positions, and theories of emotion have begun to emerge in which cognitive, biological, cultural and social processes interact within the individual. The theory of 'emotives' developed by William Reddy both retains a core universal dimension while suggesting that emotional expression is largely learned.[15] From a different disciplinary perspective, the linguist Zoltán Kövecses undertook a comparative analysis of the figurative language and metaphorical domains associated with specific emotions. Describing his approach as the 'embodied cultural prototype view', he seeks to demonstrate that emotion is 'both motivated by the human body, and produced by a particular social and cultural environment'.[16] Both these approaches suggest fruitful directions for future research into the history and cultural expression of emotion.

In conclusion, where is cultural history heading? It is always risky attempting to predict future directions, but there are indications that both structuralist, determinist perspectives, and the emphasis upon language, are in the process of being tempered by new theories giving greater weight to human creativity and practice.[17] These developments reflect the reaction against the static conceptualization of culture as a system of symbols, and a return to the idea that culture also includes intentional actions, contradiction, conflict, and transformative change.[18] The metaphor of structure appears to be giving way to new perspectives that emphasize the active and creative dimensions, the 'constructiveness', of the human mind and social communicative processes.

Constructivism as a theory became particularly influential within cognitive and social psychology and discourse theory in the later decades of the twentieth century, although many of its central ideas have a long history in European intellectual thought.[19] One of the key theorists is Frederic Bartlett, whose approach to remembering was explored in Chapter 5. The central feature of constructivism is its focus upon the ways in which individuals and communities actively create their understandings of the world around them, and it 'emphasizes the . . . generative, organizational, and selective nature of human perception, understanding and memory – the theoretical "building" metaphor guiding thought and inquiries.'[20] Constructivism encompasses both individual and collective processes of construction, and leaves open a role for active human agency.[21]

Evidence of this turn towards constructivism may be found in the recent identification of a 'performative turn' within historical writing.[22] The concept of social interaction as performance can be linked to two particular theoretical developments in the 1950s. The American sociologist Erving Goffman developed a 'dramaturgical' analysis of everyday life, adopting a theatrical metaphor to describe social encounters.[23] At around the same time an English philosopher, John Austin proposed a new approach to human speech that coalesced around the idea of 'performative utterances', statements that made things happen.[24] The dramaturgical model of human social behaviour and communication had wide disciplinary influence, and the ideas behind it converged in the concept of 'performance'. Increasingly, all aspects of human culture are perceived through the lens of performance, from rituals and festivals to the performance of identities or emotions. The difference between the older dramaturgical model and the newer concept of performance lies in the greater fluidity of the latter: 'the notion of a fixed cultural "script" is on the way out, to be replaced by the idea of improvisation, or, better, "semi-improvisation"'.[25] Pierre Bourdieu, for example, was greatly influenced by both Goffman and Austin, and his conceptualization of human social and cultural life as 'regulated improvisation' bears that imprint. Cultural historians are moving towards a perspective that acknowledges the interplay between cultural systems and cultural practices, and in the process appear to be re-engaging with the social sciences.

But two persistent problems remain: the first concerning the validity of cultural interpretation, and the second relating to the capacity for individual agency. Dilthey's questions about the epistemological validity of historical understanding and interpretation are as relevant now as they were in the nineteenth century. In 1997 Roger Chartier responded to the authors of a recently published book on historical theory and method by asking the same question: 'what are the criteria by which a historical discourse – always a knowledge based on traces and signs – can be held to be a valid and explicative reconstruction . . . of the past reality it has defined as its object?'[26] The nature of historical epistemology was the subject of intense debate among historians during the 1990s, but without resolution. In terms of individual agency, the goal for cultural historians remains the same: to find ways to describe how 'history can be culturally ordered without being culturally prescribed'.[27] A new rapprochement with the social sciences may generate innovative perspectives on both these enduring problems.

# Further Reading

▶ **Introduction and Conclusion**

Raymond Williams, *Culture and Society 1780–1950* (Harmondsworth, [1958] 1963) traces the idea of culture as it developed in Britain from 1780 to 1950. See also Williams, *Keywords* (London, [1976] 1983) for the etymology of 'culture'. For an excellent discussion of the meanings of culture by a leading literary theorist, see Terry Eagleton, *The Idea of Culture* (Oxford, 2000). A broad review of the history of cultural history may be found in Peter Burke, *What is Cultural History?* (Cambridge, 2004). The perspectives of key figures in the adoption of literary, anthropological and linguistic cultural theories from the 1980s onwards may be found in: Roger Chartier, *Cultural History* (Ithaca, NY, 1988); Lynn Hunt, ed., *The New Cultural History* (Berkeley, CA, 1989); and Victoria E. Bonnell and Lynn Hunt, eds, *Beyond the Cultural Turn* (Berkeley, CA, 1999). The latter includes a chapter by William H. Sewell that provides a comprehensive overview of 'The Concept(s) of Culture'. For a contexualized analysis of the shift from social history to cultural history, see Geoff Eley, 'Between Social History and Cultural Studies: Interdisciplinarity and the Practice of the Historian at the End of the Twentieth Century', in Joep Leerssen and Ann Rigney, eds, *Historians and Social Values* (Amsterdam, 2000), pp. 93–110. A valuable collection of chapters reflecting upon the implications of the 'linguistic turn', particularly the 'Introduction', may be found in Gabrielle M. Spiegel, *Practicing History: New Directions in Historical Writing after the Linguistic Turn* (New York, 2005). And finally, the developing interest in culture as performance and practice is explored in Richard Biernacki, 'Language and the Shift from Signs to Practices in Cultural Inquiry', *History and Theory*, 39 (2000), pp. 289–310; and Andreas Reckwitz, 'Towards a Theory of Social Practices: a Development in Culturalist Theorizing', *European Journal of Social Theory*, 5: 2 (2002), pp. 243–63.

▶ **Chapter 1**

Burckhardt discussed his approach to historical research and writing at the beginning of both *The Civilization of the Renaissance in Italy* (London, [1860] 1990), and

*The Greeks and Greek Civilisation*, edited by Oswyn Murray (London, 1998). In a series of lectures, published after his death, Burckhardt expands upon his view of historical practice: see *Judgments on History and Historians* (Boston, [1929] 1958). Recent studies of Burckhardt and his social and cultural context include Richard Sigurdson, *Jacob Burckhardt's Social and Political Thought* (Toronto, 2004), and Lionel Gossman, *Basel in the Age of Burckhardt* (Chicago, 2000). Felix Gilbert, *History: Politics or Culture?* (Princeton, NJ, 1990) considers the key debates among nineteenth-century historians. Dilthey's writings have been progressively published in Rudolf Makkreel and Frithjof Rodi, eds, *Wilhelm Dilthey: Selected Works* (Princeton, NJ, 1966). For his essays on hermeneutics, see in particular volume IV: *Hermeneutics and the Study of History*. A clear introduction to the complexity of Dilthey's thought may be found in H. P. Rickman, *Dilthey Today: A Critical Appraisal of the Contemporary Relevance of His Work* (New York, 1988). Finally, Johan Huizinga outlined his inclusive view of cultural history in 'The Task of Cultural History', *Men and Ideas: History, the Middle Ages, the Renaissance* (London, 1960). The vividness of his writing is evident in *The Waning of the Middle Ages: A Study of the Forms of Life, Thought and Art in France and the Netherlands in the XIVth and XVth Centuries* (Harmondsworth, [1924] 1965).

## ▶ Chapter 2

A great deal has been written about the *Annales* and the concept of *mentalités*. For a short introduction, see Peter Burke, *The French Historical Revolution: The Annales School, 1929–89* (Stanford, CA, 1990). A comprehensive collection of articles on the subject may be found in Stuart Clark, *The Annales School: Critical Assessments*, 4 vols (London, 1999), in particular, volumes II and IV. See also French historians Roger Chartier, *Cultural History: Between Practices and Representations* (Ithaca, NY, 1988) and Michel Vovelle, *Ideologies and Mentalities* (Cambridge, 1990). But nothing beats reading the originals: Marc Bloch, *The Royal Touch* (London, 1973), and Lucien Febvre, *The Problem of Unbelief in the Sixteenth Century: The Religion of Rabelais* (Cambridge, MA, 1982). For a critical assessment of the work of Philippe Ariès, see Patrick H. Hutton, *Philippe Ariès and the Politics of French Cultural History* (Boston, MA, 2004). Moving on to psychoanalysis and history, the two classic texts are Peter Loewenberg, *Decoding the Past: The Psychohistorical Approach* (New York, 1983), and Peter Gay, *Freud for Historians* (Oxford, 1985). For a sympathetic but critical perspective, see Timothy Ashplant, 'Fantasy, Narrative, Event: Psychoanalysis and History', *History Workshop Journal*, 23 (1987), and 'Psychoanalysis in Historical Writing', *History Workshop Journal*, 26 (1988). An influential article on the implications of psychoanalytic theory for feminist cultural history is Sally Alexander, 'Women, Class and Sexual Differences in the

1830s and 1840s: Some Reflections on the Writing of a Feminist History', *History Workshop Journal*, 17 (1984). Two older, but excellent, historical studies are Philip Greven, *The Protestant Temperament: Patterns of Child-Rearing, Religious Experience, and the Self in Early America* (New York, 1977); and John Putnam Demos, *Entertaining Satan: Witchcraft and the Culture of Early New England* (Oxford, 1982).

## ▶ Chapter 3

The complete writings of Karl Marx and Frederick Engels may be found in both electronic and print form: *The Collected Works of Karl Marx and Frederick Engels*, 50 volumes (New York, London and Moscow, 1975– ). For Antonio Gramsci, see *Selections from the Prison Notebooks* (New York, 1971); and David Forgacs and Geoffrey Nowell-Smith, eds, *Antonio Gramsci: Selections from Cultural Writings* (London, 1985). In *Marxism and Literature* (Oxford, 1977) Raymond Williams provides definitions of key concepts, such as 'culture' and 'language', analyses key concepts of Marxist cultural theory, and outlines his theory of cultural material-ism. For a classic study on the impact of writing and print upon consciousness, see Walter J. Ong, *Orality and Literacy* (London, [1982] 2002). E. P. Thompson, *The Making of the English Working Class* (Harmondsworth, [1963] 1968) has been referred to extensively in the chapter – for another example of Thompson's cultur-alist approach see *Customs in Common* (Harmondsworth, [1991] 1993). The femi-nist critique may be found in Joan Scott, *Gender and the Politics of History* (New York, 1988) which includes two important essays: 'On Language, Gender, and Working Class History' and 'Women in *The Making of the English Working Class*'. Another influential article in this debate was Sally Alexander, 'Women, Class and Sexual Differences in the 1830s and 1840s: Some Reflections on the Writing of a Feminist History', *History Workshop*, 17 (Spring 1984), pp. 125–49. Two useful studies of the British Marxist historians are Dennis Dworkin, *Cultural Marxism in Postwar Britain* (Durham, 1997), and Harvey J. Kaye, *The British Marxist Historians* (Cambridge, 1984). To trace the linguistic turn within Marxist historiography, see Gareth Stedman Jones, *Studies in English Working Class History 1832–1982* (Cambridge, 1983), and Patrick Joyce, *Visions of the People: Industrial England and the Question of Class 1848–1914* (Cambridge, 1991). Patrick Joyce, ed., *Class* (Oxford, 1995) contains a collection of readings on the concept of class, from Marx to recent poststructuralist approaches. The first British historian to draw attention to the value of anthropological approaches was Keith Thomas, 'History and Anthropology', *Past and Present*, 24 (1963). Symbolic anthropology is best under-stood by reading Clifford Geertz, *Interpretation of Cultures* (London, 1975), and Robert Darnton, 'The Symbolic Element in History', *Journal of Modern History*, 58 (1986), pp. 218–34. Excellent anthologies on the implications of cultural anthropology for historical theory and practice from the 1980s onwards are Theodore Rabb and Robert Rotberg, eds, *The New History: The 1980s and Beyond* (Princeton, NJ, 1982), and Sherry B. Ortner, ed., *The Fate of 'Culture': Geertz and Beyond* (Berkeley, CA, 1999). For an application of symbolic anthropology to a very different historical period and place, see Inga Clendinnen, 'Yucatec Maya Women and the Spanish Conquest: Role and Ritual in Historical Reconstruction', *Journal of Social History*, 15: 3 (Spring 1982), pp. 427–42. Pierre Bourdieu's writing style is not very accessible, but his theorization of 'practice' and 'habitus' may be found in *Outline of a Theory of Practice* (Cambridge, 1977). Craig Calhoun has an excellent introduction to the work of Pierre Bourdieu in George Ritzer, *The Blackwell Companion to Major Social Theorists* (Oxford, 2000). An equally good critique may be found in William H. Sewell, Jr, *Logics of History: Social Theory and Social Transformation* (Chicago, 2005).

▶ **Chapter 4**

Key texts in the development of gender theory are Joan Kelly, *Women, History and Theory: The Essays of Joan Kelly* (Chicago, 1984); Joan Wallach Scott, *Gender and the Politics of History* (New York, 1988); Judith Bennett, 'Feminism and History', *Gender and History*, 1 (1989); Kathleen Canning, 'Feminist History after the Linguistic Turn: Historicizing Discourse and Experience', in *Signs: Journal of Women in Culture and Society*, 19, 2 (1994); and Leonore Davidoff, Keith McClelland and Eleni Varikas, eds, *Gender and History: Retrospect and Prospect* (Oxford, 2000). Hayden White has developed his ideas on narrative in *Tropics of Discourse: Essays in Cultural Criticism* (1978); *The Content of the Form: Narrative Discourse and Historical Representation* (1987) and 'Historical Emplotment and the Problem of Truth', in S. Friedlander, ed., *Probing the Limits of Representation: Nazism and the 'Final Solution'* (Cambridge, 1992). A good introduction to structuralism may be found in John Sturrock, *Structuralism*, 2nd edn (Oxford, 2003), and for linguistic structuralism, see Carol Sanders, ed., *Saussure* (Cambridge, 2004). There is an extensive literature on poststructuralism/postmodernism in relation to historical theory: Elizabeth A. Clark, *History, Theory, Text: Historians and the Linguistic Turn* (Cambridge, MA, 2004) covers most of the ground. A useful introduction to Foucault may be found in Sara Mills, *Michel Foucault* (London, 2003); and a range of perspectives, in Garry Gutting, *The Cambridge Companion to Foucault* (Cambridge, 2005). The major works by Michel Foucault are: *Madness and Civilization* (1962); *The Birth of the Clinic: An Archaeology of Medical Perception* (1975); *Discipline and Punish* (1977); and *History of Sexuality*, 3 vols (1978–86). Diverse histories reflect the influence of poststructuralism, for example: Richard Price, *Alabi's World* (Baltimore, MD, 1990); Roy Porter, *Mind Forg'd Manacles: A History of Madness in England from the Restoration to* the Regency (London, 1987); Judith Walkowitz, *City of Dreadful Delight: Narratives of Sexual Danger in Late Victorian London* (London, 1992); and Diane Purkiss, *The Witch in History: Early Modern and Twentieth-Century Representations* (London, 1996). Postcolonial studies originated with Edward Said, *Orientalism: Western Conceptions of the Orient* (London, 1995). For a broad introduction to postcolonial history, see Robert Young, *Postcolonialism: An Historical Introduction* (Oxford, [1978] 2001). An excellent anthology examining the links between race, gender and power may be found in Catherine Hall, ed., *Cultures of Empire: A Reader* (New York, 2000).

## ▶ Chapter 5

Douwe Draaisma, *Why Life Speeds Up as You Get Older* (Cambridge, 2004), provides an excellent introduction to the understanding of autobiographical memory in contemporary psychology. The neuroscience of memory in general is explained in Steven Rose, *The Making of Memory: From Molecules to Mind* (London, 1992), and Daniel L. Schacter, *Searching for Memory: The Brain, The Mind, and The Past* (New York, 1996). The key early theorist in memory studies is Maurice Halbwachs, *The Collective Memory*, translated by Francis Ditter and Vida Ditter (New York, [1950] 1980), or *On Collective Memory* (Chicago, 1992). The importance of social context in remembering is further discussed in Susannah Radstone, ed., *Memory and Methodology* (Oxford, 2000), and Elizabeth Tonkin, *Narrating our Pasts: The Social Construction of Oral History* (Cambridge, 1992). The role of myth is explored in Raphael Samuel and Paul Thompson, *The Myths We Live By* (London, 1990), and Julie Cruikshank, *Life Lived Like a Story* (Lincoln, NE, 1990). For further discussion concerning narrative and composure in oral history see Mary Chamberlain and Paul Thompson, eds, *Narrative and Genre* (London, 1998), and Alistair Thomson, *Anzac Memories: Living with the Legend* (Melbourne, 1994). Interesting insights into the influence of gender upon life narrative may be found in Sherna Berger Gluck and Daphne Patai, *Women's Words: The Feminist Practice of Oral History* (New York, 1991), and Personal Narratives Group, *Interpreting Women's Lives* (Bloomington, IN, 1989). Major works in oral history include Luisa Passerini, *Fascism in Popular Memory: The Cultural Experience of the Turin Working Class* (Cambridge, 1987); and Alessandro Portelli, *The Death of Luigi Trastulli and Other Stories: Form and Meaning in Oral History* (New York, 1991) and *The Battle of Valle Giulia: Oral History and the Art of Dialogue* (Madison, 1997). An excellent anthology of key texts may be found in Robert Perks and Alistair Thomson, *The Oral History Reader*, 2nd edn (London, 2006).

## ▶ Chapter 6

Representations of history in the visual media are discussed in: Robert A. Rosenstone, *Vision of the Past: The Challenge of Film to our Idea of History* (Cambridge, MA, 1998); Tony Barta, ed., *Screening the Past: Film and the Representation of History* (Westport, CT, 1998); and Marcia Landy, ed., *The Historical Film: History and Memory in Media* (New Brunswick, 2001). See also Natalie Zemon Davis, *Slaves on Screen: Film and Historical Vision* (Cambridge, MA, 2000). The three key texts identifying the growth of a 'memorial culture' are David Lowenthal, *The Past is a Foreign Country* (Cambridge, 1985); Pierre Nora, *Realms of Memory: Rethinking the French Past*, 3 vols (New York, 1996–8); and Raphael Samuel, *Theatres of Memory*, vol. 1: *Past and Present in Contemporary Culture* (London, 1994). From an anthropological perspective, see Paul Connerton, *How Societies Remember* (New York, 1989). The relationship between the nation-state and collective memory is explored in: Benedict Anderson, *Imagined Communities: Reflections on the Origin and Spread of Nationalism* (London, [1983] 1991); Victor Roudometof, *Collective Memory, National Identity, and Ethnic Conflict* (Westport, CT, 2002); Anthony Smith, *Myths and Memories of the Nation* (Oxford, 1999); John Bodnar, *Remaking America: Public Memory, Commemoration and Patriotism in the Twentieth Century* (Princeton, NJ, 1992); and John R. Gillis, *Commemorations: The Politics of National Identity* (Princeton, NJ, 1994). A classic anthology on customs and traditions is Eric Hobsbawm and Terence Ranger, eds, *The Invention of Tradition* (Cambridge, 1983). For a specific focus upon the remembrance of war, see Jay Winter, *Sites of Memory, Sites of Mourning: The Great War and Modern Memory* (Cambridge, 1995), and James E. Young, *The Texture of Memory: Holocaust Memorials and Meaning* (New Haven, CT, 1993). An excellent older critical study of museum practice is Robert Lumley, ed., *The Museum Time-Machine: Putting Cultures on Display* (London, 1988); for more recent perspectives, see Sharon Macdonald and Gordon Fyfe, eds, *Theorizing Museums: Representing Identity and Diversity in a Changing World* (Oxford, 1996).

# Glossary

**Agency**   The idea that individuals are equipped with the ability to understand and control their own actions and shape the direction of their lives.

**Aporia**   Literally 'an unpassable path': refers to the perplexity induced by groups of statements that are individually plausible, but inconsistent or contradictory when taken in conjunction.

**Archaeology of knowledge**   The emergence of discursive formations and the underlying episteme that unites them.

**Bourgeois**   The capitalist middle class. A master, employer, or merchant.

*Bricolage*   The cobbling together of cultural forms to create new myths and stories.

**Close reading**   A method of analysis involving careful step-by-step explication of a text in order to understand how various elements work together.

**Deconstruction**   The close reading of texts in order to demonstrate that any given text has irreconcilably contradictory meanings, rather than being a unified, logical whole.

**Deduction**   Reasoning from the general to the particular.

**Diachronic**   The study of change over time.

**Empiricism**   The search for knowledge by observation and experiment.

**Epistemology**   Theories of knowledge; how we know what we know.

**Etymology**   The study of the origins of words.

**Existentialism**   An individualist philosophical and literary movement which holds that individuals are totally free and responsible for their acts.

**Gender**   The socially constructed notions of femininity and masculinity, in contrast to sex, defined as biological difference.

**Genre**   Criteria-based categories of literary composition.

**Heteroglossia**   A mixture of languages, multiplicity and diversity of voices; the simultaneous use of different kinds of speech or other signs, the tension between them, and their conflicting relationship within one text.

**Idealism**   The theory that everything exists only in the mind. The opposite of materialism.

**Identity**   Adoption of personal or collective self-image and/or social roles.

**Ideology**   The ideas, ideals, beliefs, values, political philosophies and moral justifications; belief systems which can be used to mobilize people for action.

**Induction**   Reasoning from the particular to the general.

**Materialism**   The theory that everything that is real can be experienced through the senses. The opposite of idealism.

**Metaphor**   Common figure of speech that transfers the meaning of a name or descriptive phrase to an object by analogy or substitution.

**Myth**   In Durkheim's usage myth represents a projection of social patterns upward onto a superhuman level that sanctions and stabilizes the secular ideology. A traditional narrative of anonymous authorship that arises out of a culture's oral tradition and that portrays gods and heroes engaged in epochal actions and decisions.

**Narrative**   A discursive literary style used by historians to depict sequences of change in the human past.

**Nationalism**   The feeling of belonging to a group united by common racial, linguistic and historical ties, and usually identified with a particular territory; a corresponding ideology which exalts the nation-state as the ideal form of political organization with an over-riding claim on the loyalty of its citizens.

**Ontology**   The study of the nature of reality, of what exists. Materialism and idealism are two opposing ontological theories.

**Paradigm**   A model; specifically a coherent tradition of scientific research.

**Parapraxes**   Coming out with the wrong name, embarrassing slips of the tongue; Freudian slips.

**Performatives**   A form of speech in which the issuing of the utterance is also the performance of an action.

**Positivism**   The doctrine that the goals and methods of natural science can be transferred to historiography.

**Reception Theory**   Examines the reception of a work, how the work has been viewed or understood by readers.

**Relativism**   A type of historical scepticism that holds that reliable knowledge of the past is unattainable because every work of history is inevitably limited by the subjective viewpoint of its author.

**Representation**   A representation of an event is not the event itself but a statement about or rendition of that event.

**Semiology**   The science of signs, including all sign systems such as images and gestures, as well as language. A sign is anything that conveys information to others who understand it on the basis of a system of codes and conventions they have consciously learned or unconsciously internalized as members of a certain culture.

**Subaltern**   All those groups that have been made subordinate in terms of class, caste, age, gender, or in any other way.

**Symbol**   A person, place or thing in a narrative that suggests meanings beyond its literal sense.

**Synchronic**   The study of something at a particular point in time.

**Syncretic**   The fusion of incompatible elements.

**Thick description**   A term coined by the British philosopher Gilbert Ryle; thick description moves beyond neutral observation in order to capture the layers of meaning and implications inherent in speech or gesture.

**Transcendental idealism**   A movement that flourished in the United States in the middle of the nineteenth century; a religious philosophy that emphasizes individual intuition and conscience.

**Trope**   Figures of speech, primarily metaphor, metonymy, synecdoche and irony.

## List of Sources

Bullock, Alan and Stephen Trombley, *The New Fontana Dictionary of Modern Thought,* 3rd edn (London, 1999).

Duranti, Alessandro, *Key Terms in Language and Culture* (Oxford, 2001).

Harmon, William, *A Handbook to Literature,* 10th edn (Princeton, NJ, 2006).

Kennedy, X. J., Dana Gioia and Mark Bauerlein, *The Longman Dictionary of Literary Terms* (New York, 2006).

Kirby, David, *Dictionary of Contemporary Thought* (London, 1984).

Macey, David, *The Penguin Dictionary of Critical Theory* (London, 2000).

Munslow, Alun, *The Routledge Companion to Historical Studies* (London, 2000).

Murfin, Ross and Supryia M. Ray, *The Bedford Glossary of Critical and Literary Terms* (Boston, 1997).

Ritter, Harry, *Dictionary of Concepts in History* (Westport, CT, 1986).

# Notes

► **Notes to Introduction**

1   Peter Burke, *Varieties of Cultural History* (New York, 1997), p. 1.
2   See Peter Burke, *What is Cultural History?* (Cambridge, 2004).
3   E. P. Thompson, *Customs in Common* (London, [1991] 1993), p. 13.
4   The following discussion is based upon Raymond Williams, *Keywords* (London, [1976] 1983), pp. 87–93; and Raymond Williams, *Culture* (London, 1981), pp. 10–14.
5   Williams, *Keywords,* p. 90.
6   Williams, *Culture,* pp. 11–12.
7   See Richard Biernacki, 'Method and Metaphor after the New Cultural History', in Victoria Bonnell and Lynn Hunt, ed., *Beyond the Cultural Turn* (Berkeley, CA, 1999), pp. 67–8.
8   Roger Chartier, *Cultural History* (Ithaca, NY, 1988), p. 48.
9   Terry Eagleton, *The Idea of Culture* (Oxford, 2000), p. 5.
10  J. Clifford, 'Orientalism', *History and Theory,* 19: 2 (1980), pp. 209–10.
11  Ludmilla Jordanova, *History in Practice* (London, 2000), p. 42.
12  Richard and Fernande DeGeorge, eds, *The Structuralists: From Marx to Lévi-Strauss* (New York, 1972), p. xi.
13  Ibid., p. xii.
14  Carol Sanders, 'Introduction', in Sanders, ed., *Saussure* (Cambridge, 2004), p. 2.
15  Terry Eagleton, *Literary Theory: An Introduction,* 2nd edn (Oxford, [1983] 1996), pp. 82–5.
16  See Donald R. Kelley, 'The Old Cultural History', *History of the Human Sciences,* 9: 3 (August 1996), pp. 101–26; Peter Burke, *What is Cultural History?*, pp. 7–10.
17  Burke, *What is Cultural History?*, p. 4.
18  Roger Chartier, *Cultural History: Between Practices and Representations* (Ithaca, NY, 1988), pp. 24–5.
19  Cited in Marvin Harris, *Cultural Anthropology,* 3rd edn (New York, 1991), p. 9.

20  Keith Thomas, 'History and Anthropology', *Past and Present*, 24 (1963), pp. 3–24.

21  Adam Kuper, *Culture: The Anthropologists' Account* (Cambridge, MA, 1999), p. 57.

22  James Clifford, *The Predicament of Culture: twentieth-century Ethnography, Literature and Art* (Cambridge, MA, 1988), p. 232.

23  See Miguel A. Cabrera, *Postsocial History: An Introduction* (Lanham, MA, 2004), p. 37; and review by S. Rigby, 'History, Discourse, and the Postsocial Paradigm: a Revolution in Historiography?', *History and Theory*, 45 (2006), p. 114.

24  Raymond Williams, *Marxism and Literature* (Oxford, 1977), pp. 40–1.

25  The expression comes from Alessandro Portelli, 'Narrative Form in Autobiography and Oral History', in *The Battle of Valle Giulia* (Madison, 1997), p. 86.

26  Carlo Ginzburg, *The Cheese and the Worms* (London, [1976] 1992), p. xi.

27  Mark Poster, *Cultural History and Postmodernity* (New York, 1997), pp. 10–11.

28  Jerrold Seigel, 'Problematizing the Self', in Bonnell and Hunt, *Beyond the Cultural Turn*, p. 285.

29  Wulf Kansteiner, 'Finding Meaning in Memory: a Methodological Critique of Collective Memory Studies', *History and Theory*, 41 (2002), p. 196.

30  Andrew Milner and Jeff Browitt, *Contemporary Cultural Theory*, 3rd edn (London, 2002), p. 239.

31  See Bonnell and Hunt, 'Introduction', *Beyond the Cultural Turn*, p. 1.

32  Paul Ricoeur, *The Conflict of Interpretations: Essays in Hermeneutics* (Evanston, 1974), p. 13.

33  Catherine Gallagher and Stephen Greenblatt, *Practicing New Historicism* (Chicago, 2000), p. 8.

▶ **Notes to Chapter 1     *Zeitgeist* and Hermeneutics**

1  Peter Novick, *That Noble Dream: The 'Objectivity Question' and the American Historical Profession* (Cambridge, 1988).

2  See Georg G. Iggers and Harold T. Parker, eds, *International Handbook of Historical Studies* (Westport, CT, 1979), p. 3.

3  Joyce Appleby, Lynn Hunt and Margaret Jacobs, *Telling the Truth about History* (New York, 1994), p. 71.

4  Iggers and Parker, *International Handbook*, p. 5.

5  Malcolm Kitch, 'Jacob Burckhardt: Romanticism and Cultural History', in William Lamont, ed., *Historical Controversies and Historians* (London, 1998), p. 139.

6   Felix Gilbert, *History: Politics or Culture? Reflections on Ranke and Burckhardt* (Princeton, NJ, 1990), p. 93.

7   Hugh Trevor-Roper, 'Jacob Burckhardt', *Proceedings of the British Academy,* vol. LXX (Cambridge, 1984), pp. 362–3.

8   Ibid., p. 140.

9   Richard Drake, 'Burckhardt, Jacob', in Kelly Boyd, ed., *Historians and Historical Writing* (London, 1999), p. 151.

10   Trevor-Roper, 'Jacob Burckhardt', pp. 364–5.

11   John Martin, 'Inventing Sincerity, Refashioning Prudence: the Discovery of the Individual in Renaissance Europe', *American Historical Review,* December 1997, p. 1309.

12   In a travel book, *Der Cicerone* (1855), and in *Die Geschichte der Renaissance in Italien* (1867), on architecture.

13   F. R. Ankersmit, *Historical Representation: Cultural Memory in the Present* (Stanford, CA, 2001), p. 19.

14   Jacob Burckhardt, *The Civilization of the Renaissance in Italy* (London, 1990), p. 98.

15   Jacob Burckhardt, *The Greeks and Greek Civilisation,* translated by Sheila Stern (London, 1998), p. 4.

16   Ibid., p. 6.

17   E. H. Gombrich, 'Prolusion', in Alison Brown, ed., *Languages and Images of Renaissance Italy* (Oxford, 1995), p. 2.

18   This translation from the initial paragraph of Burckhardt, *The Civilization of the Renaissance,* is cited in E. H. Gombrich, *In Search of Cultural History* (Oxford, 1969), p. 19.

19   Burckhardt, *The Greeks and Greek Civilization,* p. 7.

20   Gombrich, *In Search of Cultural History,* p. 14.

21   Frederick C. Beiser, 'Hegel's Historicism', in Beiser, ed., *The Cambridge Companion to Hegel* (Cambridge, 1993), p. 274.

22   See Peter Singer, *Hegel* (Oxford, 1983), p. 45, regarding the complexities of translating the term *Geist.*

23   Gombrich, *In Search of Cultural History,* pp. 24, 32.

24   Jacob Burckhardt, *Reflections on History* (London, 1943), pp. 85–6.

25   Ibid., p. 50

26   Ibid., p. 33.

27   Haydn White, *Metahistory: The Historical Imagination in Nineteenth-Century Europe* (Baltimore: 1973), pp. 245, 249.

28   Jacob Burckhardt, *The Civilization of the Renaissance in Italy,* vol. II (New York, 1958), p. 442.

29   John Martin, 'Inventing Sincerity', p. 1341.

30 White, *Metahistory*, p. 234.
31 Erich Heller, *The Disinherited Mind* (London [1952] 1971), p. 76.
32 See Christopher Janaway, *Schopenhauer* (Oxford, 1994), and White, *Metahistory*, pp. 237–44.
33 Cited in White, *Metahistory*, p. 235.
34 Bryan Magee, *The Philosophy of Schopenhauer* (Oxford, [1983] 1997), pp. 73–4.
35 See ibid., p. 109; Janaway, *Schopenhauer*, p. 23.
36 Janaway, *Schopenhauer*, p. 11.
37 White, *Metahistory*, pp. 238–9.
38 Ibid., pp. 232–3.
39 Ibid., p. 233.
40 Heller, *Disinherited Mind*, pp. 76–7.
41 Ibid., p. 84.
42 Burckhardt, *The Greeks and Greek Civilization*, p. 12.
43 Burckhardt, *Reflections*, p. 176.
44 Wilhelm Dilthey, 'On Jacob Burckhardt's *The Civilization of the Renaissance in Italy* (1862), in Rudolf A. Makkreel and Frithjof Rodi, eds, *Wilhelm Dilthey: Selected Works*, vol. IV (Princeton, NJ, 1996), 'Hermeneutics and the Study of History', pp. 20, 274.
45 Note that *Introduction to the Human Sciences* is also translated as *Introduction to the Human Studies*: see explanation in Makkreel and Rodi, vol. IV, 'Preface', p. vii.
46 H. P. Rickman, *Dilthey Today: A Critical Appraisal of the Contemporary Relevance of His Work* (New York, 1988), pp. 12–13, x.
47 Makkreel and Rodi, vol. IV, 'Preface', p. vii.
48 Ilse N. Bulhof, *Wilhelm Dilthey: A Hermeneutic Approach to the Study of History and Culture* (The Hague, 1980), p. 193.
49 Rickman, *Dilthey Today*, p. 21.
50 Makkreel and Rodi, vol. IV, 'The Rise of Hermeneutics', p. 236.
51 Bulhof, *Wilhelm Dithey*, p. 55.
52 Makkreel and Rodi, vol IV, 'The Rise of Hermeneutics', p. 248.
53 Makkreel and Rodi, vol. IV, 'Introduction', p. 11.
54 Cited in Rickman, *Dilthey Today*, pp. 44, 108.
55 Raymond Martin, 'The Essential Difference between History and Science', *History and Theory*, vol. 36, 1 (February 1997), pp. 1, 14.
56 Michael Ermarth, *Wilhelm Dithey: The Critique of Historical Reason* (Chicago, 1978), pp. 265–6.
57 Cited in Makkreel and Rodi, vol. IV, 'Introduction', p. 15.
58 Rudolf A. Makkreel, *Dilthey: Philosopher of the Human Studies* (Princeton, NJ, 1975), p. 25.

59 Cited in Peter Loewenberg, 'Why Psychoanalysis Needs the Social Scientist and the Historian', in Geoffrey Cocks and Travis L. Crosby, *Psycho/History* (New Haven, CT, 1987), p. 38.

60 Ermarth, *Wilhelm Dithey*, p. 246.

61 Ibid., p. 324.

62 Makkreel, *Dilthey*, pp. 346–7.

63 Ermarth, *Wilhelm Dithey*, p. 326.

64 Makkreel, *Dilthey*, p. 352.

65 Cited in Rickman, *Dithey Today*, p. 23.

66 There are different approaches within the hermeneutic tradition: see Gayle L. Ormiston and Alan D. Schrift, eds, *The Hermeneutic Tradition: From Ast to Ricoeur* (New York, 1990).

67 Rickman, *Dithey Today*, p. 56.

68 Bulhof, *Wilhelm Dithey*, pp. 69, 203; for Dilthey's critique of Schleiermacher, see Ormiston and Schrift, pp. 14–15.

69 Bulhof, *Wilhelm Dithey*, p. 69.

70 Ibid., pp. 69, 70.

71 Terry Eagleton, *Literary Theory: An Introduction,* 2nd edn (Oxford, [1983] 1996), p. 64.

72 Rickman, *Dithey Today*, pp. 7, 70–3.

73 Ibid., pp. 26, 28–9.

74 Quentin Skinner, 'Meaning and Understanding in the History of Ideas', *History and Theory,* 8: 1 (1969).

75 Karl Simms, *Paul Ricoeur* (London, 2003), p. 34.

76 See Jürgen Habermas, *Knowledge and Human Interests* (London, [1968] 1972); Rickman, *Dithey Today*, p. 74.

77 Catherine Gallagher and Stephen Greenblatt, *Practicing New Historicism* (Chicago, 2000), p. 6.

78 Stephen J. Greenblatt, *Learning to Curse* (New York, 1990), p. 5.

79 Gallagher and Greenblatt, *Practicing New Historicism*, p. 9.

80 Ibid., p. 16; Eagleton, *Literary Theory*, pp. 197–8.

81 Makkreel and Rodi, vol. IV, 'Reminiscences on Historical Studies at the University of Berlin', p. 389; Makkreel, *Dilthey*, p. 3.

82 Cited in Ernst Breisach, *Historiography, Ancient, Medieval and Modern*, 2nd edn (Chicago, 1994), p. 233.

83 Johan Huizinga, 'The Task of Cultural History', in *Men and Ideas: History, the Middle Ages, the Renaissance* (London, 1960), pp. 65–6.

84 Johan Huizinga, *The Waning of the Middle Ages: A Study of the Forms of Life, Thought and Art in France and the Netherlands in the XIVth and XVth Centuries* (Harmondsworth, [1924] 1965), pp. 15, 19, 10.

85   See F. R. Ankersmit, *Historical Representation: Cultural Memory in the Present* (Stanford, CA, 2001), p. 19.

86   Robert Anchor, 'History and Play: Johan Huizinga and his Critics', *History and Theory*, 27 (1978), p. 67.

87   Patrick H. Hutton, 'The History of Mentalities: the New Map of Cultural History', in Stuart Clark, ed., *The Annales School: Critical Assessments* ([1981] London, 1999), p. 382.

## ▶ Notes to Chapter 2   *Mentalités* and the Unconscious

1   Stuart Clark, 'The *Annales* Historians', in Quentin Skinner, ed., *The Return of Grand Theory in the Human Sciences* (Cambridge, 1985), pp. 180–1; Lawrence D. Walker, 'A Note on Historical Linguistics and Marc Bloch's Comparative Method', *History and Theory*, 19, (1980), p. 155.

2   Cited in André Burguière, 'The Fate of the History of *Mentalités* in the *Annales*', in Stuart Clark, ed., *The Annales School: Critical Assessments* 4 vols, vol. II ([1982] London, 1999), p. 409.

3   Cited in Peter Burke, *The French Historical Revolution: The Annales School, 1929–89* (Stanford, CA, 1990), p. 2.

4   Carole Fink, *Marc Bloch: A Life in History* (Cambridge, 1989), p. 90.

5   Peter Burke, *Varieties of Cultural History* (Ithaca, NY, 1997), p. 163.

6   Clark, 'The *Annales* Historians', p. 181.

7   Michel Vovelle points out that historians have had considerable difficulty in translating the term into other languages: 'German historians have tried to find an equivalent,' he wrote, 'while English historians, following the example of the Italians, have, for practical purposes, resigned themselves to using the French word.' See Vovelle, *Ideologies and Mentalities* (Cambridge, [1982] 1990), p. 4.

8   See Peter Gay, *Freud for Historians* (Oxford, 1985), p. 177.

9   Patrick Hutton, 'The History of Mentalities: the New Map of Cultural History', in Stuart Clark, ed., *The Annales School: Critical Assessments*, vol. II (London and New York, 1999), p. 382; originally published in *History and Theory*, vol. 20 (1981), pp. 237–59.

10  Cited in Roger Chartier, *Cultural History: Between Practices and Representations* (Ithaca, NY, 1988), p. 24.

11  Ibid., pp. 24–5, 28.

12  Burke, *Varieties of Cultural History*, p. 162.

13  Burke, *The French Historical Revolution*, p. 17; Marc Bloch, *The Royal Touch* (London, 1973), p. 5; this book also broke new ground as comparative history.

14   Bloch, *The Royal Touch,* pp. 1–2.

15   Robert Alun Jones, 'Émile Durkheim', in George Ritzer, ed., *The Blackwell Companion to Major Social Theorists* (Oxford, 2000), p. 239.

16   Bloch, *The Royal Touch,* p. 12.

17   Ibid., pp. 43, 41.

18   Ibid., p. 47

19   Ibid., p. 48

20   Ibid., pp. 239–42.

21   Ibid., pp. 238, 243.

22   See Hildred Geertz, 'An Anthropology of Religion and Magic, I', *Journal of Interdisciplinary History,* 6: 1 (1975), pp. 71–89.

23   Lucien Febvre, *The Problem of Unbelief in the Sixteenth Century: The Religion of Rabelais* (Cambridge, MA, 1982), p. 5.

24   Ibid., p. 336.

25   Hutton, 'The History of Mentalities', pp. 384–5.

26   Febvre, *The Problem of Unbelief,* p. 461.

27   Hutton, 'The History of Mentalities', pp. 384–5.

28   Febvre, *The Problem of Unbelief,* p. 461.

29   Ibid., p. 352.

30   David Wootton, 'Lucien Febvre and the Problem of Unbelief in the Early Modern Period', *Journal of Modern History,* 60: 4 (December 1988), pp. 702–3.

31   H. L. Wesseling, 'The *Annales* School and the Writing of Contemporary History', in Clark, ed., *The Annales School: Critical Assessments,* vol. II, p. 234.

32   Ferdinand Braudel, *The Mediterranean and the Mediterranean World in the Age of Philip II,* vol 1, 2nd edn (London, 1972), pp. 38–47; see discussion in Anna Green and Kathleen Troup, *The Houses of History: A Critical Reader in Twentieth-century History and Theory* (Manchester, 1999), pp. 87–109.

33   Vovelle, *Ideologies and Mentalities,* pp. 5–6.

34   Hutton, 'The History of Mentalities', p. 386.

35   Ibid., p. 386.

36   Chartier, *Cultural History,* p. 26.

37   Patrick H. Hutton, *Philippe Ariès and the Politics of French Cultural History* (Boston, 2004), pp. 2, 10.

38   See Hutton, *Philippe Ariès,* chapter 6: 'Decades of Debate about *Centuries of Childhood*'.

39   Hutton, 'The History of Mentalities', p. 387.

40   Cited in Vovelle, *Ideologies and Mentalities,* p. 155.

41   Burke, *Varieties of Cultural History,* pp. 170–1.

42   Chartier, *Cultural History,* p. 36.

43   Vovelle, *Ideologies and Mentalities,* p. 8.

44 Burke, *Varieties of Cultural History*, p. 176.

45 Peter Gay, *Freud for Historians* (Oxford, 1985), pp. 13–14.

46 Ibid., pp. 17–18.

47 Pamela Thurschwell, *Sigmund Freud* (London, 2000), pp. 5–7, 16.

48 Carl E. Schorske, *Fin-de-Siècle Vienna: Politics and Culture* (New York, [1961] 1979), pp. xviii, 185–6.

49 This point is made by T. G. Ashplant, 'Psychoanalysis in Historical Writing', *History Workshop Journal*, 26 (1988), p. 111.

50 Schorske, *Fin-de-Siècle Vienna*, p, 203.

51 Eli Zaretsky, 'Bisexuality, Capitalism and the Ambivalent Legacy of Psychoanalysis', *New Left Review*, 223 (May/June 1997), p. 70.

52 Thurschwell, *Sigmund Freud*, pp. 7–8; for a full list of Freud's research and publications, see Peter Gay, ed., *The Freud Reader* (London, 1995), pp. xxxi–xlvii.

53 Thurschwell, *Sigmund Freud*, p. 3.

54 Sigmund Freud, 'The Unconscious', in Peter Gay, ed., *The Freud Reader* (London, 1995), p. 573.

55 Philip Pomper, *The Structure of Mind in History: Five Major Figures in Psychohistory* (New York, 1985), p. 29.

56 Timothy Ashplant, 'Fantasy, Narrative, Event: Psychoanalysis and History', *History Workshop Journal*, 23 (Spring 1987), p. 168.

57 Thurschwell, *Sigmund Freud*, p. 51.

58 Sally Alexander, 'Women, Class and Sexual Differences in the 1830s and 1840s: Some Reflections on the Writing of a Feminist History', *History Workshop*, 17 (Spring 1984), p. 132.

59 Thurschwell, *Sigmund Freud*, p. 59.

60 Ashplant, 'Fantasy, Narrative, Event', p. 168.

61 Jeffrey Moussaieff Masson, *The Assault on Truth: Freud's Suppression of the Seduction Theory* (New York, [1984] 1985), p. 189.

62 Ashplant, 'Fantasy, Narrative, Event', p. 169; Ashplant, 'Psychoanalysis', p. 109; Gay, *Freud for Historians*, p. 117.

63 Gay, *Freud for Historians*, p. 133.

64 Ashplant, 'Psychoanalysis', p. 109; Geoffrey Cocks and Travis L. Crosby, *Psycho/History: Readings in the Method of Psychology, Psychoanalysis, and History* (New Haven, CT, 1987), p. xi.

65 Janet Sayers, *Kleinians: Psychoanalysis Inside Out* (Cambridge, 2000), pp. 17, 21–3.

66 Rosalind Minsky, *Psychoanalysis and Culture: Contemporary States of Mind* (Cambridge, 1998), p. 33.

67 Cited in Gay, *Freud for Historians*, p. 83.

68  Ibid., p. 97.

69  Pomper, *The Structure of Mind in History*, p. 81.

70  Erik H. Erikson, *Childhood and Society*, 2nd edn (New York, [1950] 1963), p. 108.

71  Pomper, *The Structure of Mind in History*, p. 83.

72  Peter Loewenberg, *Decoding the Past: The Psychohistorical Approach* (New York, [1969] 1983), p. 24.

73  Gay, *Freud for Historians*, pp. 183–4.

74  Erik H. Erikson, *Young Man Luther* (London, 1958), pp. 75, 241.

75  Ibid., pp. 252, 249.

76  Mark U. Edwards, 'Erikson, Experimental Psychology, and Luther's Identity', in Peter Homans, ed., *Childhood and Selfhood: Essays on Tradition, Religion, and Modernity in the Psychology of Erik H. Erikson* (Lewisburg, 1978), p. 94.

77  Loewenberg, *Decoding the Past*, p. 25.

78  Lyndal Roper, *Witch Craze: Terror and Fantasy in Baroque Germany* (New Haven, CT, 2004), p. 10.

79  Lyndal Roper, *Oedipus and the Devil: Witchcraft, Sexuality and Religion in Early Modern Europe* (London, 1994), p. 210.

80  Roper, *Oedipus and the Devil*, pp. 203, 211.

81  Roper, *Witch Craze*, pp. 58–9.

82  Roper, *Oedipus and the Devil*, p. 32.

83  Norbert Elias, *The Civilizing Process: The History of Manners* (Oxford, [1939] 1978).

84  Ibid., pp. 53–4, 71–4.

85  Ibid., p. 137.

86  Norbert Elias, *The Civilizing Process: State Formation and Civilization* (Oxford, [1939] 1982), p. 284.

87  Ibid, pp. 284–5.

88  Chartier, *Cultural History*, p. 91.

▶ **Notes to Chapter 3    From Agency to Symbols**

1  The following discussion draws upon 'Marxist Historians', in Anna Green and Kathleen Troup, *The Houses of History* (Manchester, 1999), pp. 34–6.

2  Peter Singer, *Marx* (Oxford, 1980), pp. 1–6.

3  Karl Marx and Frederick Engels, *The German Ideology, Part One*, ed. C. J. Arthur (New York, 1970), p. 48.

4  Karl Marx and Frederick Engels, *Selected Works* (New York, 1968), p. 182.

5  Eric Hobsbawm, 'Marx and History', in *On History* (London, 1997), p. 162.

6  David Forgacs and Geoffrey Nowell-Smith, eds, *Antonio Gramsci: Selections*

*from Cultural Writings* (London, 1985), Introduction, p. 13.

7   'Questions of Culture', *Avanti!*, 14 June 1920, in *Selections from Cultural Writings*, p. 41.

8   'Philanthropy, Good Will and Organization', *Avanti!*, 24 December 1917, in *Selections from Cultural Writings*, p. 25.

9   In contrast to contemporary anthropologists: see Kate Crehan, *Gramsci, Culture and Anthropology* (London, 2002).

10  'Observations on Folklore: Giovanni Crocioni', in *Selections from Cultural Writings*, p. 189.

11  Antonio Gramsci, 'The Intellectuals: the Formation of the Intellectuals', *Selections from the Prison Notebooks* (New York, 1971), p. 12.

12  Raymond Williams, *Marxism and Literature* (Oxford, 1977), p. 110.

13  Antonio Gramsci, 'The Study of Philosophy: Some Preliminary Points of Reference', *Selections from the Prison Notebooks*, pp. 323–4.

14  Raymond Williams, 'Culture is Ordinary', reprinted in A. Gray and J. McGuigan, eds, *Studying Culture: An Introductory Reader* (London, 1993), pp. 5–6.

15  Raymond Williams, *Marxism and Literature* (Oxford, 1977), p. 5.

16  Ibid., *Marxism and Literature*, p. 87; Harvey J. Kaye, *The British Marxist Historians* (Cambridge, 1984), p. 235.

17  Williams, *Marxism and Literature*, pp. 131–2.

18  See Perry Anderson, 'Origins of the Present Crisis', *New Left Review*, 23 (January–February 1964), pp. 26–53; Tom Nairn, 'The English Working Class', *New Left Review*, 24 (March–April 1964), pp. 43–57; and Richard Johnson, 'Thompson, Genovese, and Socialist-Humanist History', *History Workshop Journal*, 6 (1978).

19  E. P. Thompson, *The Making of the English Working Class* (Harmondsworth, [1963] 1976), p. 9.

20  E. P. Thompson, 'The Long Revolution 1', *New Left Review*, 9 (May–June 1961), pp. 32, 33.

21  E. P. Thompson, *The Poverty of Theory* (New York, 1978), p. 9.

22  Ibid., p. 88.

23  Ibid., p. 103.

24  Perry Anderson, *Arguments within English Marxism* (London, 1980), pp, 26–9.

25  E. P. Thompson, 'The Politics of Theory', in Raphael Samuel, ed., *People's History and Socialist Theory* (London, 1981), p. 406; Dennis L. Dworkin, *Cultural Marxism in Postwar Britain* (Durham, NC, 1997), p. 238.

26  Joan Wallach Scott, *Gender and the Politics of History* (New York, 1988), pp. 76, 75.

27  Alexander, 'Women, Class and Sexual Differences in the 1830s and 1840s: Some Reflections on the Writing of a Feminist History', *History Workshop*, 17 (Spring 1984), p. 131; Carolyn Steedman, *Landscape for a Good Woman* (London, [1986] 2003), p. 14.

28  Steedman, *Landscape for a Good Woman*, p. 9.

29  Ibid., p. 13.

30  Gareth Stedman Jones, *Languages of Class: Studies in English Working Class History, 1832–1982* (Cambridge, 1983), p. 101.

31  Ibid., pp. 21–2.

32  See Bryan Palmer, *Descent into Discourse: The Reification of Language and the Writing of Social History* (Philadelphia, 1990).

33  Maria Lúcia G. Pallares-Burke, *The New History: Confessions and Conversations* (Cambridge, 2002), p. 19.

34  See G. A. Cohen, *Karl Marx's Theory of History: A Defence*, 2nd edn (Oxford, [1978] 2000).

35  This discussion is based upon Jack Goody, 'Technologies of the Intellect', in *The Power of the Written Tradition* (Washington, 2000), pp. 132–51. These arguments were first formulated in Jack Goody and Ian Watt, 'The Consequences of Literacy', *Comparative Studies in Society and History*, 5 (1963), pp. 304–45. A critique of the Goody/Watt thesis may be found in Brian V. Street, *Literacy in Theory and Practice* (Cambridge, 1984), and Goody's response, in 'Objections and Refutations', *The Power of the Written Tradition*, pp. 4–9. See also Walter J. Ong, *Orality and Literacy* (London, [1982] 2002).

36  See Elizabeth Eisenstein, *The Printing Press as an Agent of Change*, 2 vols (Cambridge, 1979).

37  See Randall Collins, *Four Sociological Traditions* (Oxford, 1994); Adam Kuper, *Anthropology and Anthropologists: The Modern British School*, rev. edn (London, 1983).

38  The first British historian to draw attention to the value of anthropological approaches was Keith Thomas, 'History and Anthropology', *Past and Present*, 24 (1963), pp. 3–24.

39  Natalie Zemon Davis, 'Anthropology and History in the 1980s', in Theodore Rabb and Robert Rotberg, eds, *The New History: The 1980s and Beyond* (Princeton, NJ, 1982), p. 267.

40  Talcott Parsons, 'An Approach to the Sociology of Knowledge', in *Sociological Theory and Modern Society* (New York, 1967), pp. 139–65; William H. Sewell, 'The Concept(s) of Culture', in Victoria E. Bonnell and Lynn Hunt, eds, *Beyond the Cultural Turn* (Berkeley, CA, 1999), p. 43.

41  Clifford Geertz, *The Interpretation of Cultures* (New York, 1973), p. 89.

42  Ibid., p. 5.

43 Ibid., p. 24.

44 Ibid., pp. 208–9.

45 Sherry B. Ortner, 'Introduction', in Ortner, ed., *The Fate of 'Culture': Geertz and Beyond* (Berkeley, CA, 1999), p. 3.

46 Geertz, *The Interpretation of Cultures*, p. 9; Stephen Greenblatt, 'The Touch of the Real', in Sherry B. Ortner, ed., *The Fate of 'Culture': Geertz and Beyond* (Berkeley, CA, 1999), p. 16. Greenblatt cites Gilbert Ryle, 'Thinking and Reflecting' and 'The Thinking of Thoughts: What is "Le Penseur" Doing?' in *Collected Papers*, vol. 2: *Collected Essays, 1929–1968* (London, 1971), pp. 465–96.

47 Geertz, *The Interpretation of Cultures*, p. 17.

48 Ortner, *The Fate of 'Culture'*, p. 5.

49 Geertz, *The Interpretation of Cultures*, p. 12.

50 This argument is drawn from William H. Sewell, Jr, 'Geertz, Cultural Systems, and History: From Synchrony to Transformation', in Sherry B. Ortner, *The Fate of 'Culture': Geertz and Beyond* (Berkeley, CA, 1999), pp. 35–55.

51 Geertz, *The Interpretation of Cultures*, chapter 3.

52 Ibid., pp. 42–5.

53 Sewell, 'Geertz, Cultural Systems, and History', p. 45.

54 Geertz, 'Deep Play: Notes on the Balinese Cockfight', in *The Interpretation of Cultures*, pp. 412–53.

55 Ibid., pp. 449–50.

56 Bennett M. Berger, *An Essay on Culture* (Berkeley, CA, 1995), p. 11.

57 Ortner, *The Fate of 'Culture'*, p. 4.

58 Robert Darnton, *The Great Cat Massacre and Other Episodes in French Cultural History* (New York, 1985), pp. 77–8.

59 Ibid., p. 96.

60 Ibid., p. 100.

61 See Roger Chartier, 'Text, Symbols and Frenchness', *Journal of Modern History*, 57 (1985), pp. 682–95; Robert Darnton, 'The Symbolic Element in History', *Journal of Modern History*, 58 (1986), pp. 218–34; Harold Mah, 'Suppressing the Text: the Metaphysics of Ethnographic History in Darnton's Great Cat Massacre', *History Workshop Journal*, 31 (1991), pp. 1–20.

62 Chartier, *Cultural History*, pp. 101–07.

63 Dominick LaCapra, 'Chartier, Darnton, and the Great Symbol Massacre', *Journal of Modern History*, 60 (1988), p. 103.

64 Geertz, *The Interpretation of Cultures*, p. 24.

65 Ibid., p. 20.

66 Darnton, 'The Symbolic Element in History', p. 231.

67 Lynn Hunt, *Politics, Culture, and Class in the French Revolution* (Berkeley, CA, 1984), pp. 10–13, 54.

68 Ibid., p. 32.
69 Ibid., p. 221.
70 See Gary Alan Fine and Philip Manning, 'Erving Goffman', in George Ritzer, ed., *The Blackwell Companion to Major Social Theorists* (Oxford, 2000), pp. 468–9.
71 Pierre Bourdieu, *Outline of a Theory of Practice* (Cambridge, 1977), p. 72.
72 Craig Calhoun, 'Pierre Bourdieu', in *The Blackwell Companion to Major Social Theorists*, p. 712.
73 William H. Sewell, Jr, *Logics of History: Social Theory and Social Transformation* (Chicago, 2005), p. 139.

▶ **Notes to Chapter 4    Semiotics and Discourse**

1 See Peter Novick, *That Noble Dream: The 'Objectivity Question' and the American Historical Profession* (Cambridge, 1988). See also Joyce Appleby, Lynn Hunt and Margaret Jacob, *Telling the Truth about History* (New York, 1994).
2 See Geoff Eley, 'Is All the World a Text? From Social History to the History of Society Two Decades Later', in Gabrielle M. Spiegel, *Practicing History: New Directions in Historical Writing after the Linguistic Turn* (New York, 2005), p. 39, 44.
3 Kathleen Canning, 'Feminist History after the Linguistic Turn: Historicizing Discourse and Experience', *Signs: Journal of Women in Culture and Society*, 19: 2 (1994), p. 370.
4 Eley, 'Is All the World a Text?', pp. 43–4.
5 This discussion draws upon the chapter 'The Question of Narrative', in Anna Green and Kathleen Troup, *The Houses of History* (Manchester, 1999), pp. 204–13.
6 Dominick LaCapra, *Rethinking Intellectual History: Texts, Contexts, Language* (Ithaca, NY, 1983), p. 72.
7 Hayden White, 'The Burden of History', *History and Theory*, 2 (1966), p. 111.
8 Hayden White, *Metahistory: The Historical Imagination in Nineteenth-century Europe* (Baltimore, MD, 1973), pp. 1–42.
9 Ibid., p. ix.
10 Ibid., pp. 31–8.
11 David Macey, *Penguin Dictionary of Critical Theory* (London, 2000), p. 397.
12 Hans Kellner, 'A Bedrock of Order: Hayden White's Linguistic Humanism', *History and Theory Beiheft*, 19 (1980), p. 14.
13 F. R. Ankersmit, *Historical Representation* (Stanford, CA, 2001), p. 71.
14 Ibid., see pp. 64–8.
15 Gabrielle M. Spiegel, 'Introduction', in *Practicing History: New Directions in Historical Writing after the Linguistic Turn* (New York, 2005), p. 2.

16  Jacques Ehrmann, *Structuralism* (New York, 1970), p. ix.

17  John Sturrock, *Structuralism*, 2nd edn (Oxford, [1986] 2003), p. 27.

18  Carol Sanders, 'Introduction', in Sanders, ed., *Saussure* (Cambridge, 2004), p. 1.

19  Sturrock, *Structuralism*, p. 25.

20  John E. Joseph, 'The Linguistic Sign', in Sanders, *Saussure*, p. 61.

21  Paul Bouissac, 'Saussure's Legacy in Semiotics', in Sanders, *Sassure*, p. 240. According to Bouissac, 'both semiotics and semiology are now used with more or less the same broad value, unless specified otherwise, and cover a great variety of schools each with its own theoretical and methodological approach'. See also Risto Heiskala, *Society as Semiosis: Neostructuralist Theory of Culture and Society* (Frankfurt-am-Main, 2003).

22  Sanders, 'Introduction', p. 5.

23  Sturrock, *Structuralism*, pp. 28, 30–1.

24  Ibid., p. 36.

25  Joseph, 'The Linguistic Sign', p. 60.

26  Terry Eagleton, *Literary Theory: An Introduction*, 2nd edn (Malden, MA, [1983] 1997), p. 98.

27  Spiegel, 'Introduction', *Practicing History*, p. 6.

28  James P. Zappen, 'Mikhail Bakhtin', in Michael G. Moran and Michelle Ballif, eds, *Twentieth-Century Rhetoric and Rhetoricians: Critical Studies and Sources* (Westport, CT, 2000), pp. 7–22.

29  M. M. Bakhtin, 'The Problem of Speech Genres', in *Speech Genres and Other Late Essays* (Austin, TX, 1986), p. 84.

30  M. M. Bakhtin, 'Response to a Question from the *Novy Mir* Editorial Staff', in *Speech Genres and Other Late Essays*, pp. 6–7.

31  Eagleton, *Literary Theory*, pp. 101–2.

32  Bouissac, 'Saussure's Legacy', p. 252.

33  Claude Lévi-Strauss, *Structural Anthropology*, vol. 1 (London, 1963), p. 33.

34  Robert Deliège, *Lévi-Strauss Today: An Introduction to Structural Anthropology* (Oxford, [2001] 2004), pp. 21, 26–7.

35  Sturrock, *Structrualism*, pp. 53–4.

36  Lévi-Strauss, *Structural Anthropology*, p. 51.

37  Claude Lévi-Strauss, *The Raw and the Cooked* (London, [1964] 1970), pp. 14, 10.

38  Jack Goody, *Representations and Contradictions* (Oxford, 1997), pp. 242–4.

39  Ibid., pp. 22–3, 4.

40  Sara Mills, *Michel Foucault* (London, 2003), pp. 11–12. See also Gary Gutting, 'Introduction', in Gutting, ed., *The Cambridge Companion to Foucault* (Cambridge, 2005), p. 10 regarding the influence of Foucault's contemporary observations upon his choice of subjects.

41  Barry Smart, 'Michel Foucault', in *The Blackwell Companion to Major Social Theorists* (Oxford, 2000), p. 642.

42  Ibid., p. 631.

43  Michael Ignatieff, 'Anxiety and Asceticism', *Times Literary Supplement*, 28 September 1984, p. 1071; reprinted in Peter Burke, ed., *Critical Essays on Michel Foucault* (Aldershot, 1992), p. 71.

44  Cited in Eley, 'Is All the World a Text?', p. 38; Mills, *Michel Foucault*, p. 23. Regarding the response of historians to Foucault, see Allan Megill, 'The Reception of Foucault by Historians', *Journal of the History of Ideas*, 48 (1987), pp. 117–41.

45  Thomas Flynn, 'Foucault's Mapping of History', in Gutting, *The Cambridge Companion to Foucault*, p. 29.

46  David Macey, *The Penguin Dictionary of Critical Theory*, p. 100.

47  D. McAdam, J. D. McCarthy and M. N. Zald, *Comparative Perspectives on Social Movements* (Cambridge, 1996), pp. 6, 339; David Howarth, *Discourse* (Buckingham, 2000), p. 3.

48  Michel Foucault, *The Archaeology of Knowledge and the Discourse on Language* (New York, 1972), p. 49.

49  Victoria E. Bonnell and Lynn Hunt, 'Introduction', in Bonnell and Hunt, eds, *Beyond the Cultural Turn* (Berkeley, 1999), p. 22.

50  See Spiegel, *Practicing History*, p. 12.

51  Gareth Stedman Jones, *Languages of Class: Studies in English Working Class History, 1832–1982* (Cambridge, 1983), p. 65.

52  Macey, *Critical Theory*, p. 101.

53  David Macey, *Michel Foucault* (London, 2004), p. 73.

54  Gutting, *The Cambridge Companion to Foucault*, p. 9.

55  Macey, *Michel Foucault*, p. 74.

56  Hubert Dreyfus and Paul Rabinow, *Michel Foucault: Beyond Structuralism and Hermeneutics*, 2nd edn (Chicago, 1983), p. 18.

57  Spiegel, *Practicing History*, p. 10.

58  Michel Foucault, *Discipline and Punish* (London, 1991), p. 55; cited in Mills, *Michel Foucault*, p. 63.

59  Mills, p. 64.

60  Dreyfus and Rabinow, *Michel Foucault*, p. xxvii.

61  Michel Foucault, 'Afterword: the Subject and Power', in Dreyfus and Rabinow, *Michel Foucault*, p. 209.

62  Michel Foucault, *The History of Sexuality*, vol. 1: *An Introduction* (New York, 1978), p. 100.

63  Ibid., p. 93.

64  Macey, *Critical Theory*, p. 134.

65  Mills, *Michel Foucault*, p. 25.

66  Michel Foucault, *Madness and Civilization: A History of Insanity in the Age of Reason* (London, [1961] 1967), p. 7.

67  Dreyfus and Rabinow, *Michel Foucault*, p. 3.

68  Foucault, *Madness and Civilization*, p. 70; Mills, *Michel Foucault*, pp. 98–9.

69  Spiegel, *Practicing History*, p. 10.

70  Mills, *Michel Foucault*, p. 100.

71  Smart, 'Michel Foucault', p. 633. For new work, see, for example, Catharine Coleborne and Dolly MacKinnon, eds, *'Madness' in Australia: Histories, Heritage and the Asylum* (St Lucia, Queensland, 2003).

72  Spiegel, *Practicing History*, p. 25.

73  Lawrence E. Cahoone, ed., *From Modernism to Postmodernism: An Anthology*, 2nd edn (Malden, MA, 2003), p. 225.

74  Catherine Hall, ed., *Cultures of Empire: A Reader* (New York, 2000), p. 17.

75  Eley, 'Is All the World a Text?', p. 42; the definition is taken from the editorial in *History Workshop Journal* (1980).

76  Cited in Robert Young, *Postcolonialism: An Historical Introduction* (Oxford, 2001), p. 411.

77  Ibid., p. 416.

78  Hall, *Cultures of Empire*, p. 15.

79  Edward Said, *Orientalism: Western Conceptions of the Orient* (London, [1978] 1995), p. 3.

80  Ibid., p. 6.

81  See Ernest Gellner, 'The Mightier Pen? Edward Said and the Double Standards of Inside-out Colonialism', *Times Literary Supplement*, 19 February 1993, pp. 3–4; C. A. Bayly, 'The Indian Empire and the British Imagination', *Times Literary Supplement*, 12 July 1996, p. 29; and Robert Irwin, *Dangerous Knowledge: Orientalism and its Discontents* (Woodstock, 2006).

82  The following discussion draws upon Anna Green and Kathleen Troup, *The Houses of History* (Manchester, 1999), p. 280.

83  J. Clifford, 'Orientalism', *History and Theory*, 19: 2 (1980), pp. 209–10.

84  Hall, *Cultures of Empire*, p. 16; for an example of contradiction between discursive prescription and practice, see Ann Laura Stoler, *Carnal Knowledge and Imperial Power* (Berkeley, CA, 2002), pp. 1–2.

85  Homi K. Bhabha, 'Of Mimicry and Man: the Ambivalence of Colonial Discourse', in *The Location of Culture* (London, [1994] 2004).

86  Ibid., p. 122; Macey, *The Penguin Dictionary of Critical Theory*, p. 42.

87  See Richard White, *The Middle Ground: Indians, Empires, and Republics in the Great Lakes Region, 1650–1815* (Cambridge, 1991).

88  Natalie Zemon Davis, *Trickster Travels: A Sixteenth-Century Muslim Between Worlds* (New York, 2006), pp. 13, 110–11.

89 Eagleton, *Literary Theory*, p. 129.

90 Joan Wallach Scott, 'Gender: a Useful Category of Historical Analysis', in Scott, *Gender and the Politics of History* (New York, 1988), pp. 28–50.

91 Ibid., p. 48.

92 Mrinalini Sinha, *Colonial Masculinity: The 'Manly Englishman' and the 'Effeminate Bengali' in the Late Nineteenth Century* (Manchester, 1995), pp. 33, 35, 5.

93 Himani Bannerji, 'Politics and the Writing of History', in Ruth Roach Pierson and Nupur Chaudhuri with the assistance of Beth McAulay, *Nation, Empire, Colony: Historicizing Gender and Race* (Bloomington, IN, 1998), p. 289.

94 Kathleen Canning, 'The Body as Method? Reflections on the Place of the Body in Gender History', in Leonore Davidoff, Keith McClelland and Eleni Varikas, eds, *Gender and History: Retrospect and Prospect* (Oxford, 2000), p. 83.

95 Thomas Laqueur, *Making Sex: Body and Gender from the Greeks to Freud* (Cambridge, MA, 1990), p. 26.

96 Ibid., pp. 61–2.

97 Ibid., p. 149; Catherine Gallagher and Thomas Laqueur, *The Making of the Modern Body* (Berkeley, CA, 1987), p. viii.

98 Laqueur, *Making Sex*, pp. 151–2.

99 Ibid., p. 243. See Roy Porter's discussion of the limitations of this explanation in 'History of the Body', in Peter Burke, *New Perspectives on Historical Writing* (Cambridge, 1991), pp. 221–2.

100 Stedman Jones, *Languages of Class*, p. 67.

101 The philosopher Charles Taylor, cited in Gutting, *The Cambridge Companion to Foucault*, p. 19.

102 Ignatieff, 'Anxiety and Asceticism', p. 71; Sturrock, *Structuralism*, p. 72.

103 Elizabeth Deeds Ermarth, 'Agency in the Discursive Condition', in Spiegel, *Practicing History*, pp. 99–110.

104 Spiegel, *Practicing History*, pp. 3–4.

## ▶ Notes to Chapter 5 Remembering

1 Alon Confino, 'Collective Memory and Cultural History: Problems of Method', *The American Historical Review*, 102: 5 (December 1997), p. 1386.

2 Jay Winter and Emmanuel Sivan, *War and Remembrance in the Twentieth Century* (Cambridge, 1999), p. 1.

3 Douwe Draaisma, *Metaphors of Memory: A History of Ideas about the Mind* (Cambridge, 2000), p. 230.

4 See Larry S. Squires and Eric R. Kandel, *Memory: From Mind to Molecules* (New York, 2000), p. 215.

5  Steven Rose, *The Making of Memory: From Molecules to Mind* (London, 1992), p. 1.

6  Daniel L. Schacter, *Searching for Memory: The Brain, the Mind, and the Past* (New York, 1996), p. 5.

7  Daniel Schacter, ed., *Memory Distortion: How Minds, Brains, and Societies Reconstruct the Past* (Cambridge, MA, 1995), pp. 20–31.

8  Akiko Saito, ed., *Bartlett, Culture and Cognition* (Philadelphia, 2000), p. 3.

9  Steven Rose, 'You must remember this', *Guardian Weekly*, 14–20 January, 2005, p. 24.

10  Douwe Draaisma, *Why Life Speeds Up as You Get Older* (Cambridge, 2004), p. 1.

11  Raphael Samuel, *Theatres of Memory: Past and Present in Contemporary Culture*, vol. 1 (London, 1994), pp. 8, 18.

12  Eric Hobsbawm, *On History* (London, 1997), pp. 206–7.

13  Peter Burke, 'History as Social Memory', in Thomas Butler, ed., *Memory: History, Culture and the Mind* (Oxford, 1989), p. 98.

14  Jay Winter, 'Film and the Matrix of Memory', in *American Historical Review*, 106: 3 (June 2001), p. 860.

15  Daniel L. Schacter, *Forgotten Ideas, Neglected Pioneers: Richard Semon and the Story of Memory* (Philadelphia, 2001).

16  Alberto Rosa, 'Bartlett's Psycho-anthropological Project', in Akiko Saito, ed., *Bartlett, Culture and Cognition* (Philadelphia, 2000), pp. 49–50.

17  The following discussion draws in particular upon two key texts: Akiko Saito, ed., *Bartlett, Culture and Cognition* (Philadelphia, 2000), and Nancy Nelson Spivey, *The Constructivist Metaphor: Reading, Writing and the Making of Meaning* (San Diego, 1997).

18  U. Neisser, 'Memory: What are the Important Questions?', in M. M. Gruneberg et al., eds, *Practical Aspects of Memory* (London, 1978), pp. 3–14.

19  William F. Brewer, 'Bartlett's Concept of the Schema and its Impact on Theories of Knowledge Representation in Contemporary Cognitive Psychology', in Saito, *Bartlett, Culture and Cognition*, pp. 70–1.

20  Akiko Saito, 'Psychology as a Biological and Social Science', in Saito, *Bartlett, Culture and Cognition*, pp. 3–4.

21  Frederic Bartlett, *Remembering: A Study in Experimental and Social Psychology* (Cambridge [1932] 1995), p. 213.

22  Brewer, 'Bartlett's Concept of the Schema', p. 80.

23  Steen F. Larsen and Dorthe Berntsen, 'Bartlett's Trilogy of Memory: Reconstructing the Concept of Attitude', in Saito, *Bartlett, Culture and Cognition*, p. 92.

24  Bartlett, *Remembering*, p. 207.

25  Larsen and Berntsen, 'Bartlett's Trilogy of Memory', p. 93.

26  Bartlett, *Remembering*, p. 244.

27  Ibid., p. 266.

28  Ibid., pp. 296, 298.

29  The discussion in this paragraph is based upon Maurice Halbwachs, *The Collective Memory*, translated by Francis Ditter and Vida Ditter (New York, [1950] 1980).

30  Halbwachs, *The Collective Memory*, p. 49.

31  Ibid., p. 51.

32  Ibid., p. 48.

33  Larsen and Berntsen, 'Bartlett's Trilogy of Memory', pp. 112–13.

34  James Fentress and Chris Wickham, *Social Memory* (Oxford, 1992), p. ix.

35  Michael Schudson, 'Dynamics of Distortion in Collective Memory', in Schacter, *Memory Distortion: How Minds, Brains and Societies Reconstruct the Past*, pp. 346–47.

36  See, for example, Paul Thompson, *The Edwardians* (St Albans, 1975).

37  Most notable among these is Angela Hewins, *The Dillen* (Oxford, 1982).

38  Raphael Samuel, ed., *Miners, Quarrymen and Saltworkers* (London, 1977); Elizabeth Roberts, *A Woman's Place: An Oral History of Working-class Women, 1890–1940* (Oxford, 1984); Sherna Berger Gluck, *Rosie the Riveter* (New York, 1987).

39  Alessandro Portelli, *The Battle of Valle Giulia: Oral History and the Art of Dialogue* (Madison, 1997), pp. 293–4.

40  Luisa Passerini, 'Work Ideology and Consensus under Italian Fascism: Work in Progress', *History Workshop Journal*, 8 (1979), p. 84; also see Passerini, *Fascism in Popular Memory: The Cultural Experience of the Turin Working Class* (Cambridge and Paris, 1987).

41  Passerini, 'Work Ideology and Consensus', p. 85.

42  Ibid., p. 92.

43  Ibid., p. 104.

44  Luisa Passerini, 'Women's Personal Narratives: Myths, Experiences, and Emotions', in The Personal Narratives Group, eds, *Interpreting Women's Lives* (Bloomington, IN, 1989), p. 197.

45  Passerini, 'Work Ideology and Consensus', p. 84.

46  Ronald Grele, 'A Surmisable Variety: Interdisciplinarity and Oral Testimony', in *Envelopes of Sound*, 2nd edn (New York, 1991), pp. 159–61.

47  Ronald Grele, 'Movement without Aim: Methodological and Theoretical Problems in Oral History', in *Envelopes of Sound*, p. 143.

48  Ronald Grele, 'Listen to Their Voices: Two Case Studies in the Interpretation of Oral History Interviews', *Oral History*, 7: 1 (Spring 1979), p. 33.

49  Marie-Françoise Chanfrault-Duchet, 'Narrative Structures, Social Models, and

Symbolic Representation in the Life Story', in Sherna Berger Gluck and Daphne Patai, *Women's Words: The Feminist Practice of Oral History* (New York, 1991), p. 80.

50 Chanfrault-Duchet, p. 89.

51 Portelli, *The Battle of Valle Giulia*, p. 5.

52 S. Dentith, 'Contemporary Working-class Autobiography: Politics of Form, Politics of Content', in P. Dodd, ed., *Modern Selves: Essays on Modern British and American Autobiography* (London, 1986), pp. 69–71; T. G. Ashplant, 'Anecdote as Narrative Resource in Working Class Life Stories', in Mary Chamberlain and Paul Thompson, eds, *Narrative and Genre* (London, 1998), pp. 99–113.

53 Simon Featherstone, 'Jack Hill's Horse: Narrative Form and Oral History', *Oral History* (Autumn 1991), p. 61.

54 Elizabeth Tonkin, *Narrating Our Pasts: The Social Construction of Oral History* (Cambridge, 1992), p. 3.

55 Ibid., p. 50.

56 Anna Green, *British Capital, Antipodean Labour: Working the New Zealand Waterfront, 1915–1951* (Dunedin, 2001), pp. 77–9.

57 Alistair Thomson, *Anzac Memories: Living with the Legend* (Melbourne, 1994). See in particular the Introduction, and Appendix 1. 'Anzac' is the acronym for the Australian and New Zealand Army Corps.

58 Ibid., p. 216.

59 Raphael Samuel, 'Myth and History: a First Reading', *Oral History*, 16 (1988), p. 15.

60 See Elena Cabezali, Matilde Cuevas and Maria Teresa Chicote, 'Myth as Suppression: Motherhood and the Historical Consciousness of the Women of Madrid, 1936–9', and Rina Benmayor, Blanca Vázquez, Ana Juarbe, and Celia Alvarez, 'Stories to Live By: Continuity and Change in Three Generations of Puerto Rican Women', both in Raphael Samuel and Paul Thompson, *The Myths We Live By* (London, 1990), pp. 184–200.

61 Samuel and Thompson, *The Myths We Live By*, p. 17.

62 Luisa Passerini, 'Women's Personal Narratives: Myths, Experiences, and Emotions', p. 191.

63 Portelli, *The Battle of Valle Giulia*, pp. 7–8.

64 Jane Moodie, 'Preparing the Waste Places for Future Prosperity? New Zealand's Pioneering Myth and Gendered Memories of Place', *Oral History*, 28: 2 (Autumn 2000), p. 62.

65 Julie Cruikshank, 'Myth as a Framework for Life Stories: Athapaskan Women Making Sense of Social Change in Northern Canada', in Samuel and Thompson, *The Myths We Live By*, pp. 174–83.

66 Ibid., p. 178.

67  Susan Ostrov Weisser, '"What Kind of Life Have I Got?": Gender in the Life Story of an "Ordinary" Woman', in Sidonie Smith and Julia Watson, eds, *Getting a Life: Everyday Uses of Autobiography* (Minneapolis, 1996), p. 267.

68  Tonkin *Narrating Our Past*, pp. 104–5.

69  Ibid., p. 106.

70  Annette Wieviorka, 'From Survivor to Witness: Voices from the Shoah', in Jay Winter and Emmanuel Sivan, eds, *War and Remembrance in the Twentieth Century* (Cambridge, 1999), p. 137.

71  Lawrence L. Langer, *Holocaust Testimonies: The Ruins of Memory* (New Haven, CT: 1991), p. 201.

72  Bartlett, *Remembering*, p. 227.

73  Portelli, *The Battle of Valle Giulia,* pp. vii–viii.

74  Milan Kundera, *The Book of Laughter and Forgetting* (New York, 1999), p. 4.

## ▶ Notes to Chapter 6  Collective Memory

1  Andreas Huyssen, *Twilight Memories: Marking Time in a Culture of Amnesia* (New York, 1995), p. 5.

2  Ibid., p. 14.

3  Michel-Rolph Trouillot, *Silencing the Past: Power and the Production of History* (Boston, 1995), p. 19.

4  The term is that of Pierre Nora, *Les Lieux de mémoire* (Paris, 1984–92).

5  Michael Kammen, *Mystic Chords of Memory: The Transformation of Tradition in American Culture* (New York, 1991), p. 667. See also Marcia Landy, *Cinematic Uses of the Past* (Minneapolis, 1996); Natalie Zemon Davis, *Slaves on Screen: Film and Historical Vision* (Toronto, 2000); Tony Barta, ed., *Screening the Past: Film and the Representation of History* (Westport, CT, 1998).

6  Robert A. Rosenstone, 'The Historical Film: Looking at the Past in a Postliterate Age', in Marcia Landy, ed., *The Historical Film: History and Memory*, (New Brunswick, 2001) p. 51.

7  The term comes from Wulf Kansteiner, 'Finding Meaning in Memory: a Methodological Critique of Collective Memory Studies', *History and Theory*, 41 (May 2002), p. 182.

8  David Lowenthal, *The Past is a Foreign Country* (Cambridge, 1985), pp. xv, xvi.

9  Ibid., pp. 410, 360–1, 411.

10  Raphael Samuel, *Theatres of Memory*, vol. 1: *Past and Present in Contemporary Culture* (London, 1994), p. 169.

11  Ibid., pp. 160–1.

12  Ibid., pp. 197–8.

13  Ibid., pp. 242–3, 275, 281, 221.

14 Pierre Nora, *Realms of Memory: Rethinking the French Past*, 3 vols (New York, 1996–8); Hue-Tam Ho Tai, 'Remembered Realms: Pierre Nora and French National Memory', *American Historical Review*, 106: 3 (June 2001), p. 906.

15 Nora, *Realms of Memory*, vol 1, pp. xvii, xv.

16 Pierre Nora, 'Between Memory and History: *Les Lieux de Mémoire*', *Representations*, 26 (Spring 1989), p. 13.

17 Lawrence Kritzman, 'In Remembrance of Things French', in Nora, *Realms of Memory*, vol. 1, p. ix.

18 Ibid., p. x.

19 Nora, *Realms of Memory*, vol. 1, p. xix.

20 Hue-Tam Ho Tai, pp. 910, 915, 917, 921.

21 Samuel Hynes, 'Personal Narratives and Commemoration', in Jay Winter and Emmanuel Sivan, *War and Remembrance* (Cambridge, 1999), p. 206.

22 See also Susannah Radstone, *Memory and Methodology* (Oxford, 2000), pp. 2–9.

23 Jacques Le Goff, *History and Memory* (New York, 1992), p. 11.

24 Huyssen, *Twilight Memories*, pp. 251, 9, 260.

25 Alon Confino, 'Collective Memory and Cultural History: Problems of Method', *American Historical Review*, 102: 5 (December 1997), pp. 1386–7.

26 Maurice Halbwachs, *On Collective Memory* (Chicago, 1992), p. 37.

27 Ibid., p. 40.

28 Patrick Hutton, 'Collective Memory and Collective Mentalities: the Halbwachs–Ariès Connection', *Historical Reflections/Réflexions Historiques*, 15: 2 (1988), pp. 314–15.

29 Halbwachs, *On Collective Memory*; Hutton, 'Collective Memory and Collective Mentalities', p. 316.

30 James E. Young, *The Texture of Memory: Holocaust Memorials and Meaning* (New Haven, CT, 1993), p. xi.

31 Wulf Kansteiner, 'Finding Meaning in Memory: a Methodological Critique of Collective Memory Studies', *History and Theory*, 41 (May 2002), p. 180.

32 Jeffrey Olick, ed., *States of Memory: Continuities, Conflicts, and Transformations in National Retrospection* (Durham, 2003), p. 6.

33 See, for example, Ed Cairns and Mícheál D. Roe, eds, *The Role of Memory in Ethnic Conflict* (Basingstoke, 2003), Introduction.

34 Jan Assman, 'Collective Memory and Cultural Identity', *New German Critique*, 65 (Spring–Summer 1995), p. 128. Raphael Samuel described heritage as lexically 'capacious enough to accommodate wildly discrepant meanings', see Samuel, *Theatres of Memory*, p. 208.

35 John R. Gillis, ed., *Commemorations: The Politics of National Identity* (Princeton, NJ, 1994), p. 4.

36 Ibid., Gillis, p. 45.

37 Kammen, *Mystic Chords of Memory*, p. 688.

38 Gillis, *Commemorations*, pp. 43–9.

39 Olick, *States of Memory*, p. 1.

40 Eric Hobsbawm, 'Ethnicity and Nationalism in Europe Today', *Anthropology Today*, 8: 1 (1992), p. 3. See also Eric Hobsbawm, *Nations and Nationalism since 1780* (Cambridge, 1990).

41 Cairns and Roe, *The Role of Memory*, p. 8.

42 Olick, *States of Memory*, p. 5.

43 Benedict Anderson, *Imagined Communities: Reflections on the Origin and Spread of Nationalism* (London, [1983] 1991), pp. 4, 6.

44 Ibid., pp. 36, 7.

45 Ibid., pp. 9–10, 11–12, 163–4.

46 Eric Hobsbawm, 'Introduction: Inventing Traditions', in Eric Hobsbawm and Terence Ranger, *The Invention of Tradition* (Cambridge, 1983), pp. 12, 1.

47 Hugh Trevor-Roper, 'The Invention of Tradition: The Highland Tradition of Scotland', in Hobsbawm and Ranger, *The Invention of Tradition*, pp. 15–41.

48 Eric Hobsbawm, 'Introduction: Inventing Traditions', p. 13.

49 Eric Hobsbawm, 'Mass-producing Traditions: Europe, 1870–1914', in Hobsbawm and Ranger, *The Inventiuons of Tradition*, p. 263.

50 Anthony Smith, *Myths and Memories of the Nation* (Oxford, 1999), Preface, 12.

51 Ibid., pp. 271–4.

52 Yael Zerubavel, *Recovered Roots: Collective Memory and the Making of the Israeli National Tradition* (Chicago, 1995), pp. 12, 61–2, 68, 137, 208–9, 212.

53 Patrick J. Geary, *The Myth of Nations: The Medieval Origins of Europe* (Princeton, NJ, 2002), pp. 11–13, 37.

54 Ibid., pp. 12, 37.

55 Samuel, *Island Stories*, p. 8.

56 Jay Winter, *Sites of Memory, Sites of Mourning: The Great War in European Cultural History* (Cambridge, 1995), pp. 10–11.

57 See Paul Fussell, *The Great War and Modern Memory* (Oxford, 1975); Samuel Hynes, *A War Imagined: The Great War and English Culture* (London, 1991).

58 Winter, *Sites of Memory*, p. 5.

59 Ibid., pp. 2–3, 5, 93–4.

60 Ibid., pp. 228–9.

61 Young, *The Texture of Memory*, p. 9. See also chapter 6, 'The Biography of a Memorial Icon: Nathan Rapoport's Warsaw Ghetto Monument', pp. 155–84.

62 Kristin Ann Hass, *Carried to the Wall: American Memory and the Vietnam Veterans Memorial* (Berkeley, CA, 1998), p. 13.

63 Gillis, *Commemorations*, p. 13.

64 Hass, *Carried to the Wall*, pp. 12–17.

65  John Bodnar, *Remaking America: Public Memory, Commemoration, and Patriotism in the Twentieth Century* (Princeton, NJ, 1992), pp. 13–14, 253.

66  Hass, *Carried to the Wall*, pp. 148, 10–11, 18.

67  Jay Winter, 'Forms of Kinship and Remembrance in the Aftermath of the Great War', in Jay Winter and Emmanuel Sivan, *War and Remembrance in the Twentieth Century* (Cambridge, 1999), pp. 9, 40.

68  T. G. Ashplant, Graham Dawson and Michael Roper, eds, *The Politics of War Memory and Commemoration* (London, 2000), p. 9.

69  Ibid., pp. 43, 47.

70  Steven C. Dubin, *Displays of Power: Memory and Amnesia in the American Museum* (New York, 1999), pp. 186–226. See also Thomas F. Gieryn, 'Balancing Acts: Science, *Enola Gay* and History Wars at the Smithsonian', in Sharon Macdonald, ed., *The Politics of Display: Museums, Science, Culture* (London, 1998), pp. 197–228; Vera Zolberg, 'Museums as contested sites of remembrance: the Enola Gay affair', in Sharon Macdonald and Gordon Fyfe, eds, *Theorizing Museums: Representing Identity and Diversity in a Changing World* (Oxford, 1996), pp. 69–82.

71  Young, *The Texture of Memory*, p. xii.

72  Ashplant, Dawson and Roper, *The Politics of War Memory*, pp. 11–12, 34, 36. See also Jonathan F. Vance, *Death So Noble: Memory, Meaning, and the First World War* (Vancouver, 1997), pp. 266–7.

73  Gillis, *Commemorations*, p. 17.

74  Hass, *Carried to the Wall*, pp. 21–3, 2–3.

75  Roy Rosenzweig and David Thelen, *The Presence of the Past: Popular Uses of History in American Life* (New York, 1998), pp. 89–114.

76  Ibid., p. 184.

77  Paula Hamilton, 'Memory Studies and Cultural History', in Hsu-Ming Teo and Richard White, *Cultural History in Australia* (Sydney, 2003), p. 83.

78  Young, *The Texture of Memory*, p. 21.

## ▶ Notes to Conclusion

1  Jack Goody, in Maria Lúcia G. Pallares-Burke, *The New History: Confessions and Conversations* (Cambridge, 2002), p. 26. See this idea more fully explicated in Goody, *Representations and Contradictions* (Oxford, 1997).

2  William H. Sewell, Jr, 'The Concept(s) of Culture', in Victoria E. Bonnell and Lynn Hunt, eds, *Beyond the Cultural Turn* (Berkeley, CA, 1999), p. 50.

3  Maria Lúcia Pallares-Burke, *The New History: Confessions and Conversations* (Cambridge, 2002), p. 58.

4  M. M. Bakhtin, 'Response to a Question from the *Novy Mir* Editorial Staff', in *Speech Genres and Other Late Essays* (Austin, TX, 1986), p. 7.

5  Homi K. Bhabha, 'The Postcolonial and the Postmodern', in *The Locaton of Culture* (London, [1994] 2004), p. 246.

6  Jack Goody, 'Technologies of the Intellect', in *The Power of the Written Tradition* (Washington, 2000), p. 148.

7  The only one on this list not previously mentioned is Daniel Roche, *My Life by Jacques-Louis Ménétra* (New York, 1986).

8  Please note that 'individuality' is distinct from 'individualism', which has a specific set of meanings within political philosophy and economic theory that are not intended here.

9  Steven Rose, *The 21st Century Brain: Explaining, Mending and Manipulating the Mind* (London, 2005), p. 59.

10  See Wolf Singer, 'Consciousness from a Neurobiological Perspective', in Steven Rose, ed., *From Brains to Consciousness? Essays on the New Sciences of the Mind* (Princeton, NJ, 1998), p. 244.

11  Rose, *The 21st Century Brain*, p. 57.

12  Ibid., p. 54.

13  Peter N. Stearns with Carol Z. Stearns, 'Emotionology: Clarifying the History of Emotions and Emotional Standards', in Geoffrey Cocks and Travis L. Crosby, eds, *Psycho/history: Readings in the Method of Psychology, Psychoanalysis, and History* (New Haven, CT, 1987), p. 284.

14  Ibid., pp. 303-4.

15  William Reddy, *The Navigation of Feeling: A Framework for the History of Emotions* (Cambridge, 2001), p. xi.

16  Zoltán Kövecses, *Metaphor and Emotion: Language, Culture, and Body in Human Feeling* (Cambridge, 2000), p. 14.

17  Gabrielle M. Spiegel, *Practicing History: New Directions in Historical Writing after the Linguistic Turn* (New York, 2005), p. 18.

18  See the discussion in William H. Sewell, 'The Concept(s) of Culture', in Victoria E. Bonnell and Lynn Hunt, eds, *Beyond the Cultural Turn* (Berkeley, CA, 1999), p. 44.

19  In some contexts, the term 'constructivist' may be used in relation to individual cognitive processes, whereas 'constructionism' is applied to constructivist studies of large social collectivities. See Nancy Nelson Spivey, *The Constructivist Metaphor: Reading, Writing, and the Making of Meaning* (San Diego, 1997), p. 19.

20  Ibid., p. 3.

21  Constructivism has been criticized for a 'tendency towards voluntarism', in other words an inclination to exaggerate the extent to which people can be free agents in the constructive process. See Jeffrey K. Olick, *Continuities, Conflicts, and Transformations in National Retrospection* (Durham, 2003), p. 7.

22 Peter Burke, 'Performing History: the Importance of Occasions', *Rethinking History*, 9, 1 (2005), p. 35.

23 Erving Goffman, *The Presentation of Self in Everyday Life* (New York, 1959).

24 J. Austin, *How to Do Things with Words* (Oxford, 1962).

25 Burke, 'Performing History', p. 41.

26 See Roger Chartier, 'Introduction', in *On the Edge of the Cliff: History, Language, and Practices* (Baltimore, MD, 1997), p. 9. The book in question was Joyce Appleby, Lynn Hunt and Margaret Jacob, *Telling The Truth about History* (New York, 1994).

27 Speigel, *Practicing History*, p. 21.

# Index